# THE COMPLETE
# *PAPILLON*

## Carolyn & David Roe

Ringpress

Published by Interpet Publishing,
Vincent Lane, Dorking, Surrey,
RH4 3YX, UK.


First published 1992
Second edition published 1999
This edition printed 2003

**ISBN 1 86054 190 9**


Printed and bound in Singapore
by Kyodo Printing Co

10 9 8 7 6 5 4 3

# CONTENTS

**We dedicate this book to 'Fanta', our first Papillon, who taught us so much about this enchanting breed.**

*Ch. Fircrest Fanta Of Sunshoo.*                    *Pearce.*

# ACKNOWLEDGEMENTS

We would very much like to acknowledge and thank the people that have helped us, in one way or another, to get this book off the ground and finished!

Mrs Norma Staff has helped on many occasions, with information spanning over many years. Pat Groff in the United States has worked tirelessly for us, and Anna and Ian McKnight have helped with the research.

Graham Turnbull, the artist, worked so hard on the lovely drawings to illustrate the Breed Standard. The photographers we have used are: Di Pearce, Martin Leigh, Chris Lawrence, Don Robinson, Russell Jones, Sally Ann Thompson, David Abbot, and Alan Walker, and we would also like to thank all those in the breed that supplied photographs and information. Thanks also to Paul Keevil and Sheila Bullock of Framed Philatecs, who were a tremendous help with the chapter on Papillon Collectables.

Mike Gearry, veterinary surgeon, checked the chapter on First Aid and Veterinary Care, to make sure that we we had not forgotten all that we had learned! And finally, thanks to Val, who took charge of our boarding kennels at various times to enable the book to be completed.

# PREFACE

Dogs have always played an important part in our lives. In fact, there has never been a time when we were without a dog. Papillons are very special to us, they have such unique features in such small bodies. They are constant companions, and each one is different, not only in looks but also in personality. We have had great pleasure in owning this breed, and also in judging it, both in Britain and overseas. As a result of this we have made many friends, and this has given us an insight into dogs all over the world.

While we have been researching and writing this book we have come across some beautiful Papillons. Unfortunately, we could not include every one, but just a small selection to illustrate this charming breed. We have given our own opinion on many subjects associated with the Papillon, and we have also included as much factual information as possible. The number of Papillons is growing steadily throughout the world, and all those involved in the breed have a responsibility to safeguard its future. We hope that this book, in some small measure, will be a help to all those who strive to maintain the true type and quality of this enchanting toy dog.

*Carolyn and David Roe with some of their Sunshoo Papillons and their Maremma Sheepdog.* Pearce.

# Chapter One

# HISTORY OF
# THE PAPILLON

The Papillon is a descendant of the Continental Toy Spaniel, and this breed probably dates back to the fourteenth century. The word 'spaniel' means 'dog of Spain', but it is very difficult to trace the Papillon's precise country of origin – it has been claimed by France and Belgium as well as Spain. The popular belief is that the breed originated in France, hence the French names 'Papillon' (butterfly) for the erect-eared variety, and 'Phalene' (moth) for the drop-eared variety. The history of the Continental Toy Spaniel, the Royal Toy Spaniel and the Papillon is virtually impossible to separate in the early years; all three toy dogs were bred as companion 'lap' dogs, and they were the favourites of the nobility, who could afford to breed dogs specifically to serve their leisure pursuits. As a result, hunting dogs were bred to serve the master of the household, and toy dogs were bred to be dainty, attractive and ornamental, with a faithful and loving temperament. The best record of the Papillon's development can be found in the portraits painted of royalty and nobility over the centuries. One of the earliest paintings to feature a Papillon is *St. Anthony* by the Italian artist Sasetta (1392-1450). This is one of a series of paintings by the artist, and in this particular painting a small black and white Papillon is depicted. Tizano Vercelli, better known as Titian, painting in Italy in the sixteenth century, portrays a red and white Papillon in his beautiful painting, *The Venus of Urbino*. There is also a painting called the *Vendramin Family,* which features a Phalene. The Spanish artist Velazquez (1598-1660) painted the young Prince Philip Prosper with a lemon and white Papillon reclining in a chair; Antoine Pesne (1683-1757) painted Queen Sophia Dorothea with her charming and most dainty Phalene, and Jacob Bogdani (1660 to 1724) painted a still life with a liver and white Papillon. In France

*Two-year-old Clarissa Strozzi with her Phalene, painted in 1542 by Titian (1486-1576)*

the Papillon is first recorded in a painting commissioned by Henry IV of Navarre to mark his second marriage. The artist is Peter Paul Rubens (1577-1640) and he includes a Papillon in his painting called *Marriage of Marie de Medicis*, as well as in a later painting to commemorate the birth of the infant Prince who became Louis XIII when he was nine years old. Louis XIII married Ann of Austria, and in a portrait of the new Queen by the Flemish artist Franz Pourbus (1569-1622), the family Papillon is featured. Louis XIV succeeded to the throne when he was just five years old, and Papillons were very much a part of French court life. A black and white Papillon appears in a portrait of the King with his family by the French artist Largillere (1659-1746). The Phalene is also represented in this period with a painting by Antoine Watteau (1684-1721) in a picture called *Bei-der-Toilette*.

The first Papillon 'on the move' was created with mother-of-pearl and semi-precious stones as an ornament made for Louis XIV's bedchamber. Marie Antoinette had a model of a Phalene in Sevres porcelain, and it was found in her room after her death. She had two Papillons, and after she died at the guillotine, the inhabitants of the house took care of her pet dogs until they died. The house in Paris is now known as 'The House of the Papillon'. Madame de Pompadour, mistress of King Louis XIV, had two Papillons called Inez and Mimi, and there is an engraving called *The Faithful* by Baron Albert Houtart which shows Madame de Pompadour sitting with a Papillon on her lap.

There are a number of colourful anecdotes concerning Papillons and their royal connections.

*Queen Sophia Dorothea.   Antoine Pesne 1740.*

*Kaiser Franz Joseph and Kaiserin Maria Theresa with their children.*
                                                  *Martin van der Meytens*

King Henri III of France is reputed to have upset members of his council of state by appearing with small open baskets suspended round his neck, which were full of Papillons! Henri would go in person to Lyon, where the dogs were bred, and would pay exorbitant prices for them; in 1576 it is reported that he spent over 100,000 crowns on his beloved dogs. He had three favourite dogs, and they were allowed to sleep with him and guard him. One of these dogs was called Liline, and she was with the King in St Cloud when a monk called Jacques Clement asked for a

*This picture was painted by the Hungarian artist Jacob Bogdani, who died in England in 1724.*

*Print from an American newspaper, dated 1877, entitled 'What's That', presented to the Dog Museum in St Louis by Dr and Mrs Lola.*

royal audience. Liline took such a violent dislike to the monk that the King had to confine the dog to an ante-chamber. When the monk was left alone with the King he presented a letter and then stabbed the King in the chest. The monk tried to make his escape, but Liline and her companions barked and raised the alarm, and the monk was over-powered. It was too late for Henri III, and as he lay dying he gasped: "If only I had heeded Liline's warning."

The Papillon's fame through paintings by well known artists has spread throughout the world. American collections have a number of fine examples including Malcolm S. Tucker's *Dog with a Box*, showing a red sable Papillon, presented by Catherine D. Gauss to the Dog Museum in St Louis. There is also a delightful painting of a Papillon which appears with two little girls in a picture called *Guess Again* by Sophie Anderson, which belongs to the Forbes Magazine Collection in New York. Obviously these paintings can only present us with an artist's impression of the breed, but there is one important point that comes across in all the pictures depicting Papillons from the earliest times, and that is the honoured place the little toy dogs hold in the family. When a portrait is painted to show an individual or a family at their best – as they want to be remembered – the Papillon, the perfect companion dog, is an integral part of the scene.

# Chapter Two

# THE PAPILLON AS A COMPANION

The Papillon is an exquisitely pretty little dog from the Toy Group. As a breed, they are friendly and intelligent, and they like to please. This is a dog that thrives on human companionship, and as they are generally long-lived, they soon become an integral member of the family. Papillons are remarkably adaptable. Over the years we have seen them in many different homes and environments, and, given the right care and attention, they will be content living in anything from a small flat to a grand mansion. The aim of most Papillons is to accompany their owners everywhere they go, and fortunately, they are usually good travellers. When we go out in the car we usually put our Papillons in a travelling box for safety reasons, but they are quite happy with this arrangement, and sleep for most of the journey. However, no matter where we have been – it could be a round trip of a couple of hundred miles to attend a dog show – they always know when we are within a couple of miles of home, and they sit up and start to bark.

CHARACTER AND TEMPERAMENT

Character is really what makes a dog. We have always said that no matter how beautiful and perfect a Papillon may be according to the Breed Standard, it must, first and foremost, be a dog that you are able to live with. We believe that a good, sound temperament should be treated as a priority when breeding, just as much as the other important points of the Breed Standard. The British Breed Standard stipulates that the Papillon should be lively, intelligent, friendly, with no aggression, and always alert. It is worth examining each of these characteristics separately.

*The Papillon is a bold and lively dog, who will live in harmony with all the members of its family.*                                                    *Pearce*

LIVELY: Anyone who has owned a Papillon will tell you that this is a dog that is always on the move, dashing here and there. It is rarely content to amble along, but prefers to live life in the fast lane: rushing into the kitchen for its dinner, roaring up the hall like a whirlwind to see who is at the door, and running round and round the sitting room, just for the heck of it. Then, eventually, it collapses in a heap and falls sound asleep.

INTELLIGENT: The Papillon is a dog that likes to learn, and then to have plenty of praise for getting it right. It is able to figure out quite complicated situations, and is not averse to trying to outwit you! A number of people have been very successful with their Papillons in obedience and agility competitions, and the dogs clearly enjoy themselves. However, it takes a lot of hard work and patience to reach these high standards, although it is very rewarding. Many owners take their Papillons to local dog training classes to achieve a level of basic obedience, and to socialise with

*The Papillon should not be unduly suspicious, and should never show aggression.*

other dogs and humans. An intelligent dog is often a sensitive dog, and this is certainly the case with the Papillon. These little dogs are very aware of our moods and feelings, and just as they love to be praised, so they hate to be told off.

FRIENDLY: The Papillon is a very happy dog, and friendliness seems to come as second nature. It will give a few barks when the door bell rings, and then, when you have invited the visitor into the house, it will be only too happy to make them welcome. We are often stopped when we are out walking with our Papillons, and people comment on what delightful dogs they are. This is one of the great joys of being a dog-owner – it is amazing how many new friends you make.

WITHOUT AGGRESSION: The Papillon should never be unduly suspicious or show aggression towards people or other animals, and in our experience it is very seldom the case that it does.

ALERT: Papillons are excellent house dogs: they always hear someone coming up the path

*All Papillons are inquisitive and love to investigate their surroundings.*

*The Papillon will enjoy a day out hiking, but sometimes it prefers to take life easy.*

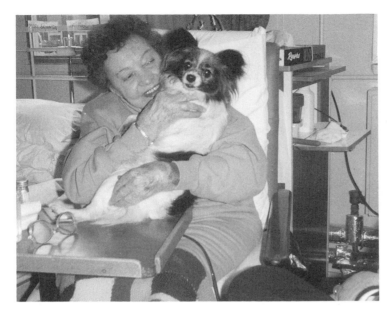

*Papillons make ideal Therapy or PAT dogs because of their size and their friendly, out-going temperament.*

before we do, and they are always aware of anything new that is happening.

The Papillon is a dog that is full of character and charm; it is cheeky, inquisitive and very affectionate. It really is the epitome of a big dog in a small dog's clothing. We cannot envisage a time when there would be no Papillons in our household – life would not be complete without them. Papillons, like most toy breeds, were bred as 'Companion Dogs', in contrast to a Labrador, for example, which was bred to retrieve game for its master. As a result, the Papillon excels at being a companion: its whole body seems to wag with excitement when it greets you, it loves to go out for a walk with you, and it is quite happy to curl up on your lap while you read a book or watch the television. The Papillon is definitely not a dog that likes to be shut out in a kennel and left for the day. The result would be a very unhappy dog. This is a fun-loving dog, with a great sense of humour. There are many different activities that you can share with your Papillon, and we can guarantee that once you have owned a Pap, you will be a convert for life!

## HIKING

Hiking or rambling is a very popular pastime, and just because the distances covered are some eight miles in a day, do not think this will over-face your Papillon. We know of one hiker who has four Papillons ranging from three years old to fifteen years, and they enjoy every minute of their walks, often out-running the Setters, Labradors and Collies.

## THERAPY DOGS

These are known as P.A.T. Dogs in Britain. This stands for Pro Dogs Active Therapy, and their work is organised through Pro Dogs National Charity. In America, therapy dogs are also playing an important role in hospitals, old people's homes and other institutions. Therapy dogs are given

*Mark Whitehill, with his Papillon Amicae Amastotter, being presented with the award for Top Junior Handler in Scotland.*

a temperament test, for it is important that they are totally trustworthy, and also that they will enjoy their work. Our Papillon Max is a registered PAT Dog, and we visit the local retirement home and hospice with him. The residents take it in turns to have Max on their laps, and to make a fuss of him. Max adores the attention, and you can see the value of his visits as he always gets everyone talking and laughing.

JUNIOR HANDLING

This is known as Junior Showmanship in the States, and it is becoming an increasingly popular competition at all the shows. Mark Whitehill handled his Papillon, Amicae Amastotter, with notable success, winning the Scottish Junior Handler of the Year in 1990. Mark says: "Papillons are not the easiest dogs to handle. You need to be on your toes, and you must have plenty of patience. When you come into the ring, concentrate on your own dog and not anybody else's. Try to relax, because if you are relaxed, this will transfer to the dog. Always remember that dog showing is fun: if you win, it is a bonus; if you don't, then there is always another show, another day."

STAGE APPEARANCES

Papillons have had a few parts in plays. Their attractive appearance coupled with their intelligence make them an ideal choice when a dog is needed in a drama. However, things do not always go according to plan. One Papillon, Ringlands Oridan, went along to audition for a production of Chekov's *The Cherry Orchard* at the National Theatre. However, Oridan kept cocking his leg on Sir Ralph Richardson's walking-stick, so the understudy, another Papillon called Rinzim Natasha, was brought in! She was more ladylike in her manners, and appeared in the production for a ten-month run. She had her own dressing-room, and of course, there was a star on the door! The Papillon, Stouravon Mint Julep of Beajoy, went into films, and appeared in the award-winning movie *Company Of Wolves*.

# Chapter Three

# CARING FOR YOUR PAPILLON

Most Papillons do not need a lot a of special care; however, the proper care is most important if you are to have a healthy and happy companion. If you are a newcomer to the breed, you will need to contact a reliable breeder – addresses are available from breed clubs and the national Kennel Club. It is important to go and see some of the Papillons that the breeder has; there is nothing like seeing and being with Papillons to make absolutely 100 per cent sure that this is the breed for you. It will also give you the opportunity to talk to the breeder and learn more about the breed. Do not be offended if the breeder asks you lots of questions. A responsible breeder will not let a dog go until they are confident that it is going to a good home, and it is a good idea to try and anticipate any problems before you take on the commitment of owning a dog. The questions most commonly asked by breeders are:

**1. Do you go out to work all day?**
It really would not be fair on a young Pap to be left alone in the house for hours on end, without any human companionship.

**2. Have you owned a toy breed before?**
A Papillon is far from being the smallest of the Toy Group, but there is awful lot of difference between taking a Papillon puppy home, compared with a Labrador puppy or a West Highland White Terrier puppy.

### 3. Are there any young children in the house?
No matter how fond of dogs children are, they can be too rough with a young puppy, so supervision is required, in handling and playing with the young puppy, and also the puppy must be allowed to sleep peacefully in between bouts of play-time.

### 4. Where will the puppy live and sleep?
A Papillon thrives on human companionship, and it would be most unhappy if it was not included as a member of the family. It will be happiest if it has a bed in the kitchen, or somewhere else in the house that is warm and draught-free.

### 5. Do you want a male or a female?
Some people are adamant about whether they want a male or female, and, of course, it is largely a question of personal preference. I would always choose a male because I think they are more affectionate than bitches, they do not come into season, and they very often carry a better coat. The disadvantage is that they do cock their leg at the drop of a hat, unless they have been properly trained. People that prefer bitches usually believe that this sex is more faithful, and they also think that they are cleaner than dogs. You may find it easier to purchase a male from a breeder, as some breeders want to keep their best bitches for breeding.

### 6. Do you plan to show your Papillon?
You must be honest with the breeder if you are hoping to purchase a Papillon to show. There is no point in saying that you want one as a pet in the hope that it will be good enough to show. However, even if the breeder selects a puppy with show potential, there is no guarantee that it will make the grade. It is often difficult to tell whether a Papillon, aged twelve weeks, has the correct physical make-up to be successful in the show ring. It is far easier to wait until the puppy is about five to six months old, and by that time you should be able to get a good idea as to how big or small it will be, if it has a good mouth, and if it is a male it should be entire by this stage. Obviously, a five- to six-month-old puppy is more expensive to buy than a twelve-week-old puppy, so this is another consideration to bear in mind.

### 7. Do you want to use your Papillon as future breeding stock?
Again, you must be fair to the breeder and explain that you are looking for a bitch to breed from or a dog to use at stud. In the same way that you cannot guarantee that a puppy will be a success in the show ring, you cannot be certain that a puppy will be capable of producing top-class offspring. However, there are certain steps you can take, such as studying the line that you want by looking at pedigrees and assessing the dogs that it has produced. Obviously, if you are planning to breed with a dog or a bitch, you must be confident that it is completely sound in its physical and mental make-up.

### 8. Why do you think a Papillon is the right breed for you?
This is quite a heart-searching question and needs a bit of thinking about. Every individual has their own personal reasons, but make sure you are clear in your own mind about why you want to own a Papillon.

Assuming that you have asked yourself all of these questions, and more, and you have

*Papillons will adapt to kennel life, but most prefer to be house pets, as they thrive on human companionship.*

*A Papillon may be allowed on the furniture, but it should also have its own bed.*

decided to go ahead with buying a Papillon puppy, the next step is to book a puppy. You will need to specify whether you want a male or a female, a show puppy or a companion, and then it is a matter of waiting until the litter is born. The breeder will probably let you come and see the puppies before they are ready to leave their mother, and most breeders will let you collect your puppy when it is about twelve weeks of age. There are a few things that you will need to get ready for the puppy's arrival.

It will need a bed to sleep in. A cardboard box is the most suitable thing at this stage. It is warm and draught-proof, but if it is chewed or soiled, it can be thrown away. You will need some bedding in the box. We always use a type of bedding that is warm and cosy for the puppy, and it washes and tumble-dries very quickly. It is a good idea to have two pieces, so you can change the bedding regularly. The puppy also needs a small water dish and a food dish, a light collar and lead, a small identity disc with the dog's pet name and your phone number, some chew-resistant toys, and few hide chews.

Most breeders provide a diet sheet, so check with the breeder to see what sort of diet she feeds, and try and keep to it for a good few days. If you want to make any changes to the diet, introduce them very gradually, otherwise the combined stress of moving from one home to another, plus a different diet, will almost certainly lead to a tummy upset. We have worked out a good, basic diet which is suitable for a puppy aged twelve weeks. There is a wide range of pet-food manufacturers to choose from, and most breeders will have found the type that suits their dogs. However, whether you feed tinned, fresh, or dried food, it must be of high quality.

PUPPY DIET

There are a large number of food products on the market and each owner and breeder has their own preference. These days, there are a lot of 'tailor-made', dry dog diets on the market, which will cover your puppy through the whole of its life. Some of these diets are excellent and well-balanced, so no additives are required at all – just fresh drinking water.

We leave down a small dish of good-quality, dry food, so that the puppies can eat when they are hungry, and we gradually cut down on the four meals a day once the puppy starts to 'pick' at one of his meals.

We cut out the supper meal first, then the lunch meal, then tea, and finally we change the breakfast to the adult diet. There are no hard-and-fast rules about the age and when to cut out a meal as it will vary from puppy to puppy.

BREAKFAST: Half a scrambled egg.

LUNCH: Good-quality, tinned puppy food (for example, a lamb-and-rice type), or sachets.

TEA AND SUPPER: As lunch.

MILK
We do not to give milk to puppies, as it tends to make them loose.

ADULT DIET

BREAKFAST: In the morning, we give some assorted biscuits to all of the Papillons.

MAIN MEAL: The main meal can be given either as one meal, or – and we think this is better – as two meals. We use dry dog food and have done so for the past eight years.

We use a 'junior' food for all dogs under seven years of age. For dogs older than seven, we use either an 'adult' or 'senior' food.

WATER
Fresh drinking water should be available at all times, for both adult dogs and puppies, whether fed a meat-based diet or a dry, complete diet.

COLLECTING YOUR PUPPY
At last, the day arrives when you are ready to collect your puppy. It is a good idea to take a small blanket or towel for the puppy to lie on in the car – or, ideally, take a travelling box. Make sure you also take some kitchen roll to mop up with in case of accidents in the car. It could be the first time that your puppy has been out in a car, and it will certainly feel very confused, leaving its brothers and sisters and going off with a complete stranger.

When you collect your puppy, the breeder will give you a diet sheet, and possibly a vaccination certificate if the puppy has had any vaccinations. If the puppy is being sold for show, the breeder must provide registration papers and a pedigree.

If it is being sold on the condition that it is purely a pet, and not to be bred from, you may not be given any documents. Responsible breeders sell a puppy without papers sometimes to prevent breeding from a particular dog or bitch for any number of reasons – usually because it has a particular fault, such as a bad mouth or a poor front – but that does not mean that the animal is not healthy or typical of the breed. A pet Papillon does not need to have papers, but it is important that the buyer understands the arrangement.

The breeder will probably be anxious to hear how the puppy settles into its new home, and it is a good idea to keep in contact, in case any problems arise. Most reliable breeders are only too happy to hear from you and to give advice, particularly if you are new to the breed.

When a puppy arrives at its new home, it is likely to feel quite overwhelmed. Give it a chance to find its way round, and to get used to its new surroundings and all the different noises and smells. There are some puppies that just bounce around, as if they have no worries at all, and there are others that need time to adapt; each puppy is an individual and no two are ever the same! For the first few days, let the puppy get used to you and its new surroundings first, and then you can start to socialise the puppy with people outside the immediate family.

## THE FIRST DAY AT HOME

Give your puppy an hour or two to settle, and then offer a small meal. Don't worry if it refuses to eat, just take the dish away after ten minutes, and offer it again a couple of hours later. Make sure there is a bowl of fresh water available, and let it have any toys that it is allowed to play with.

Remember to take the puppy into the garden every couple of hours, every time it wakes up, and after eating, to encourage it to be clean. You cannot start house-training too early. When the puppy does what is required, give plenty of praise. If it makes a mistake in the house, there is no point in telling the puppy off, unless you catch it in the act. Once the deed has been done, the puppy will not associate the reprimand with what it has done wrong. If you catch the puppy making a mess, use a stern voice to let it know that you are displeased, and then put the puppy straight out into the garden.

Papillons are usually pretty quick to learn, and as they hate to be told off, they will soon get the message.

## PLAY-TIMES

One of the golden rules with puppies of any breed is never let a puppy do something you would not allow it to do as an adult dog. This might include chewing on your fingers or trying to hang on to your slippers as you walk along. If you fail to correct this type of behaviour, you will simply be making a rod for your own back. When the puppy is ten months old, it will not understand why it is not allowed to play these sorts of 'games'.

If you want to stop a puppy doing something, say 'no' in a firm voice, and then divert its attention to a new game, or a toy that it is allowed to play with. Do not confuse a puppy with lots of different words of command; a simple 'no' is all that is required.

If you teach your puppy good manners, it will be welcome everywhere you go. You will be able to take it to other people's houses, and on holiday with you. There is so much bad publicity concerning dogs these days, we should try to create a good impression with our lovely breed.

Puppies sleep an awful lot, and these periods of rest are interspersed with energetic playtimes. A puppy will often amuse itself with all sorts of games. It likes to have a mad chase around, no one knows what it is chasing, but the puppy is determined to catch it, whatever it is. Papillon puppies look so comical haring around, tail tucked underneath, head and neck outstretched for aerodynamics, and whoosh they're off! We buy 'dog dollies' from our Papillon Club Benevolent Fund, and they make marvellous toys – the dogs adore them, wrestling with them, pouncing on them, and then picking one up and bringing it to show you, whether you want it or not! Puppies are great time-wasters, far better than the television, and then, all of a sudden, they will collapse in a heap and fall into a really deep sleep, no doubt dreaming of their next playtime.

Try to establish a routine for the puppy from day one. Dogs are great creatures of habit, and I think it makes life easier all round, if the puppy knows what to expect at a certain time – and it certainly assists with training.

VACCINATIONS

If your puppy has not been vaccinated, do not take him out in the street or park, or any place where other dogs have been. Make an appointment with your vet to take the puppy along so that it can start its course of vaccinations. Most vets will start the vaccination course from eight weeks.

When you take along your puppy for vaccinations, it is also a good idea to discuss other routine health care issues with the vet. These include whether you should have your Papillon microchipped, and also which worming product your vet recommends, although your puppy should have been wormed before leaving his breeder. You should use a good-quality worming preparation every six months.

Puppies normally have a course of two vaccinations, which are a fortnight apart. They are vaccinated against distemper, hepatitis, leptospirosis and parvovirus. The vet will usually give the puppy a general check-up before starting the course of vaccinations – there would be little point in vaccinating a sick dog. The puppy's temperature will probably be checked. This can be a degree higher than normal, if the puppy is a bit over-excited or over-awed, but this is nothing to worry about.

The vet will also check the puppy's eyes and ears, have a look in its mouth, and check to see if the puppy has any hernias. It really is not safe to let your puppy go out to meet other dogs, or go where other dogs have been, until about five days after the second vaccination. However, in the meantime, you can try a bit of lead-training in the garden, and this will make it easier when it is time to go out into the wide world.

TRAINING

Some owners like to take their dogs to obedience training classes. There are some excellent clubs, but there are some that are not as good and this can lead to problems, so ask your vet or a friend with a dog if they know of a good class in your area.

Your puppy could well be the smallest dog at the training class, so when you join the class, try to be placed next to a small, well-behaved dog, so that your dog is not frightened and distracted by a large and very boisterous dog. For some reason, Papillons will sometimes go in 'where angels fear to tread', and some have no fear of large dogs. In principle, this is as it should be; but some large dogs can be upset by a little dog running round their feet, where they can't see them, and this is when accidents happen. Large dogs do have large and heavy feet!

Some Papillons are also under the illusion that they can 'fly', and then try to launch themselves from the back of the sofa, or from the table. This is not a good idea, as if a dog lands badly, a broken leg could result. A lot of people say you should not let Papillons jump on and off furniture, or run up and down stairs, for fear of accidents, but we think that it is virtually impossible to restrict a dog to this extent. However, try to think for your Papillon and prevent it from doing anything that could prove harmful.

THE SENIOR CITIZEN

We are lucky that most Papillons live to a ripe old age, and although some start to slow down, and prefer to sleep a bit more, they need little extra care or attention. Two of our own Papillons, Fanta and Luanda, lived till they were sixteen and a half, but one outstanding little Papillon was Shimna Goldfinch, owned by Mrs Mooney. At twenty years of age, this remarkable dog won Veteran Dog at Crufts in 1991. He looked a picture, and was a real credit to his owner.

We give our seniors duvets to sleep on, which they seem to find comfortable and cosy, especially if they are prone to rheumatism. We also split their meals, and feed half their rations at lunch-time and the other half at tea-time, which seems to suit them better.

Unfortunately, a lot of older Papillons lose their teeth or have to have teeth removed by the vet. Some owners think that this means that all food should be mashed or sloppy, but this is definitely not the case. Some three weeks after teeth have been removed, the gums start to become quite hard, and it is amazing what the dog will be able to eat, such as biscuits, small chunks of meat and chew sticks. We have formulated a diet that is suitable for an older dog, and it has been fed to dogs that have been well into their teens. With the older dog, little and often is the rule.

As we said previously, we feed a 'complete' dry food for adult and veteran dogs, but if your Papillon has been fed a meat diet, you may find this helpful.

SENIOR CITIZEN DIET

BREAKFAST: Half a scrambled egg or a quarter piece of wheat-biscuit breakfast cereal mixed with a little warm water and honey.

LUNCH: A small amount of meat, either tinned, sachet or fresh, which can be mixed with a few cooked vegetables.

TEA: As lunch.

SUPPER: Half a digestive or rich tea biscuit.

As far as general care is concerned, it is really a matter of commonsense. Do not let an elderly dog stand outside in the pouring rain, or if it is really cold. Make sure it has a comfortable bed that is draught-proof, and try to keep to a routine so that it does not become confused.

An older dog will probably need to go out at more regular intervals to relieve itself. Make sure it is still groomed regularly so that its coat feels nice, and trim its nails so they do not become too long and make its toes spread.

One of our oldies lived to be sixteen years old, and remained very lively and independent. He would go off to the orchard, and would be totally deaf to our attempts to call him back – except when it was dinner-time!

30

# Chapter Four

# GROOMING

Grooming is an important part of your dog's care and well-being, whether it is a companion or a Champion; it is only the techniques that differ. We start off by looking at the grooming that a puppy and a pet Papillon requires, and then move on to the more elaborate grooming that is needed to present a Papillon in the show ring.

It is a good idea to start grooming a puppy as young as possible, from six to seven weeks of age. There may not be very much coat to groom, but it will get the puppy used to the routine, and most will come to love it. We normally start when the puppy is about six weeks old, although it will already have had its nails clipped a couple of times. Nails grow very quickly and can be sharp, so we nip the ends off using a pair of sharp scissors or guillotine nail-clippers. The first grooming session consists of running a bristle brush over the body coat, ears, tail and trousers. The puppy usually thinks this is great fun and tries to catch the brush! Try to control the puppy quietly; the aim is to get the puppy lying quietly on your lap, quite relaxed, and enjoying being brushed. If you do this on a daily basis, you will be surprised how quickly the puppy will learn to settle down, and it will start to look forward to these sessions. After about ten days, we introduce a metal comb, and we use this to go through the ear fringes and tail.

When our puppies are eight weeks old, we give them a bath. We put a rubber mat in the bottom of the bath so that the puppy will not slip, and then use a shower attachment to wet the coat. Talk to the puppy all the time to reassure it, and apply the shower gently on one part of the coat until it gets used to the experience, and then you can wet the entire coat. Do not spray its face or into its ears, and do be careful to ensure that the water is warm – never hot or cold. The skin of a Papillon puppy is very sensitive and quite delicate, so use a mild shampoo specially formulated for puppies. Then rinse the coat thoroughly, making sure that all traces of shampoo have been

*Three-month-old Papillon puppies with their ears fully erect.* *Pearce.*

rinsed away. Then take a cotton pad, moistened with warm water, and wipe over the puppy's face. Finally, take another pad of warm, wet cotton-wool (cotton) and gently wipe the inside flap of the ears. Try to remove as much excess water from the coat as possible, and then lift the puppy from the bath and wrap it in a towel. Dry the coat by gently patting or rubbing, and make sure the puppy is kept in a warm place until its coat is completely dry. Then you can give the puppy a brush and a comb, and the coat usually comes up with a beautiful pearly sheen.

As the puppy gets older, you must keep a check on the toe nails and dew claws, if there are any. Occasionally, you will need to trim the hair between the pads on the dog's feet, and we would recommend that you use safety scissors or round-ended scissors to do this. This hair should be removed, as it can easily harbour bits of debris, and if it is left unattended, it can turn into a large mat, which is most uncomfortable for the dog. In extreme cases, the volume of hair in this area can make a dog's feet spread. Every month, check the dog's ears and clean them with a solution of canine ear-cleaning drops – there are a number of different brands on the market. Put a couple of drops into each ear, massage the side of the ear gently, and then use cotton-wool (cotton) to wipe out any excess fluid or debris that comes up the ear. Do not poke about in the ear with cotton buds, as this could prove harmful and painful to the dog. If the dog's ear looks inflamed or smells, or the dog does not like you touching its ear, then a trip to the vet would be advisable.

Most Papillons are the erect-ear type, and the drop-eared Phalene is far more unusual. However, most puppies are born with their ears folded down. Sometimes they will go up quite quickly, but they can take months to go up. When this happens, many breeders or owners try to assist the ears by massaging them in the hope that this will improve the muscles and help them

*The 'ugly duckling' phase, with one ear up and one ear down, and the tail looking like a flagpole.*

to become erect. An alternative method is to put the ears in what is called 'curlers'. This is done by holding the ear erect and then putting a piece of fairly wide clear tape around the outside of the ear, and as close to the base of the ear leather as possible. This forms a kind of tube and the ear stands up. It is hoped that if the ears receive this sort of artificial support for a period of time, it will help them to become erect naturally. You must be very careful when you remove the clear tape, as it is obviously attached to the hairs on the ears, and it could be painful for the dog if it is removed too roughly. When a puppy is teething its ears will do the most peculiar things. For instance, you can have one ear going up and one ear going down. You can even have one that folds backwards, which really does look comical. This is not a cause for concern, and once the teething is finished, the ears normally revert to normal.

When you are grooming your Papillon, keep an eye out for any unwelcome visitors, such as the odd flea, which can be picked up quite easily. If you spot the tell-tale flea-dirts, or a flea itself, spray the coat with an insecticidal spray – again there are many products formulated for dogs on the market. As the puppy is growing up, remember to keep a regular check on its teeth. Some Papillons retain the occasional puppy tooth, but we tend to ignore this until the dog is about nine months old. If the tooth has not come out by then, we usually get the vet to remove it. However, be guided by what your own vet recommends. There are a variety of special toothpastes and toothbrushes that are designed for dogs, and if you get your puppy used to having its teeth cleaned from an early age, it will accept the routine quite happily. The alternative is a trip to the vet to have the teeth scaled. You can try and scale the teeth yourself, but you will have to be careful, as it is very easy to nick the dog's gum with the scaler. At some time between four and eight months, Papillon puppies lose their puppy coat, and they look absolutely awful – we always say they look like a pipe-cleaner! When a puppy starts to moult, do not be tempted to try and preserve the coat by not grooming it. Groom as normal, and then at the end of the moult give the dog a bath, and then wait for the new coat to grow in. A good quality coat needs good feeding, so it is important to feed a dog correctly. This will help to make the coat shine and look healthy. When a dog is not well its coat very often is lacklustre and dull, and the dog will start to moult.

## HOME GROOMING KIT

Bristle brush.
Wire-pin brush (it must have rounded tips).
Double-ended metal comb (one side for fine-combing of fringes, the other side with wider teeth for going through the main coat).
Nail-clippers (we prefer the guillotine type for Papillons).
Safety scissors.
Cotton wool (cotton) balls.
Ear cleaning drops.
Coat dressing, or light oil dressing.
Dog toothpaste and toothbrush.
Shampoo.
Conditioner.
Towels.

## GROOMING FOR THE SHOW RING

The same general principles apply when you are grooming for the show ring as when you are looking after a pet Papillon, and the most important of these is to start early, so that the puppy gets used to a grooming routine. You want a Papillon that is going to enjoy these sessions, rather than one that struggles and gets upset as soon as it sees a comb!

When you are grooming for the show ring, the coat and fringes are very important, so take every possible care to preserve these intact. We brush through the coat every day with a pure bristle brush, but it is not a good idea to groom a dry coat, so you will need some coat dressing or light oil, to ensure that the coat does not break. There are several products on the market, and everyone has their own preference as to which they think is the best. If you are combing through the coat, and you suddenly come to a halt, meeting an obstruction, do not pull on regardless. Examine the coat and find out what is causing the problem: it may be a small knot or a little bit of dried food. Try to tease out the tangle, very carefully. If you are still having trouble, spray with some coat dressing or de-matting liquid. Work this in gently with your fingers, and then try again to tease it out with the comb. If you are grooming regularly and using coat dressing or oil, do not let it build up in the coat, otherwise it will become sticky and greasy, so regular bathing and conditioning is required.

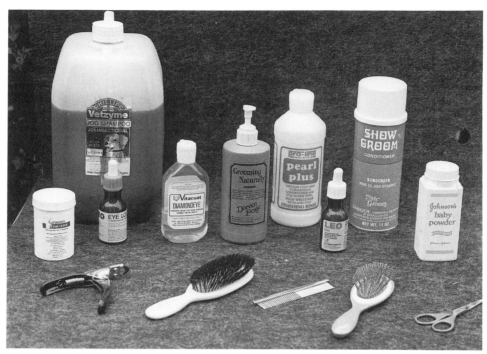

*A complete set of grooming equipment for the show dog.     Pearce.*

*After the dog has been bathed, Carolyn wraps it in a towel and attaches it to the grooming arm. Pearce.*

A grooming arm can be very useful as it leaves both hands free. However, you should never leave a dog unattended while it is attached to a grooming arm. *Pearce.*

*Start the dryer, but always point it away from the dog to begin with, so that it gets used to the noise before feeling the force of air on its body.      Pearce.*

*The advantage of using a grooming arm can be seen, as it leaves both hands free to adjust the dryer.     Pearce.*

*Dry the dog's coat in layers, starting at the bottom layer and gradually working through the coat.                    Pearce.*

To dry the tail, spread the feathering on to the table and point the dryer at the tail. Keep brushing the hair from the base or root of the tail, towards the tip. *Pearce.*

*The coat will need regular grooming – not just after a bath – and the golden rule is never to brush or comb a dry coat. The coat should first be dampened with a coat spray, or a little dressing can be sprayed directly on to the brush or comb before grooming commences.*                                   *Pearce.*

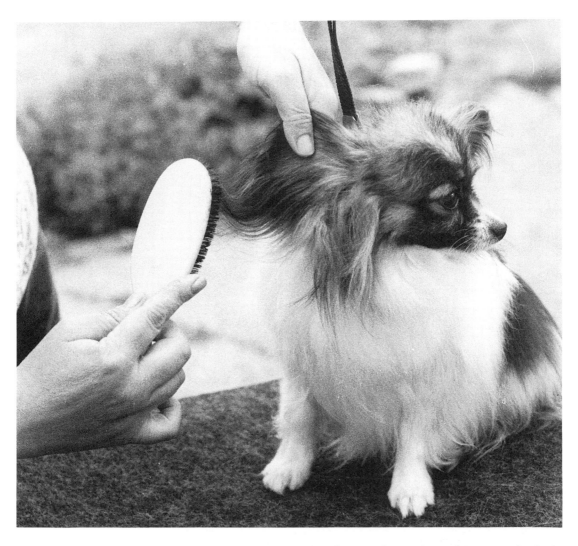

*The ear fringes must be brushed thoroughly, but be gentle, and never tug at the hair. If you meet an obstruction with the brush or comb, it should be gently teased out.*

*Pearce.*

Some Papillons suffer
from eye stain, and this
shows up as a pink stain
on the white part of the
coat, just below the
inside corner of the eye.
Regular treatment will
be needed with a special
eye-cleaning product,
and this should be
applied to a clean pad
of cotton wool, and then
wiped from the corner
of the eye in a
downwards motion. Use
a fresh pad of cotton
wool for each eye.
Pearce.

*Trim the hair that grows between the pads, otherwise it will make the foot spread. It can also become knotted and collect debris, making it most uncomfortable for the dog. Always use scissors with round ends or safety scissors.*     *Pearce*

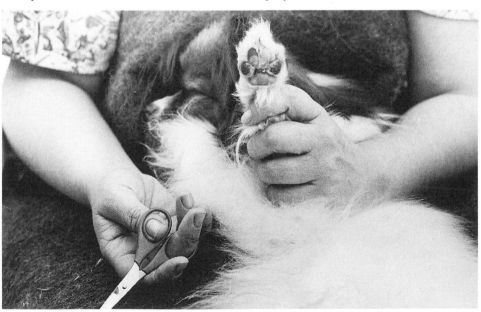

*The foot after it has been trimmed. Carolyn finds it easier to lie the dog on her lap for this job.*     *Pearce*

*Keep a regular check on the nails to make sure they do not grow too long. Carolyn uses guillotine nail-clippers, and again, she prefers to lie the dog on her lap.*

*Pearce.*

Before you bath the dog, groom through the entire coat to make sure it is tangle free. If you bath and then dry a dog that has tangles or knots in its coat, you will set the knots in even tighter. Bathe the dog in a good-quality, canine cleaning shampoo. We follow this up with a second, whitening shampoo. Then apply a conditioner and work into the coat well. Rinse thoroughly. Wrap the dog in a towel, and prepare to dry it. If its nails need to be trimmed, you can do the job at this stage, just after the bath, as the dog's nails are softer and therefore easier to trim. We have a grooming table and grooming arm, and this allows us to attach the dog to the grooming arm and leaves both hands free. We also have a stand drier, so that we can direct the drier to the area of coat that we are working on. To begin with, use a brush, and lift the coat with the brush, and then gradually brush it down, so that the coat dries straight. If the coat is not dried thoroughly, it can make it look crimpy and spoil the overall effect; so drying the coat properly is time well spent. Take special care when you are drying the ear fringes, and never use the dryer to blow direct into the dog's face – they absolutely hate this. Equally, take care not to blow hot air on to a male's testicles – understandably the dog will object to this! When you are satisfied that the dog is completely dry, go through the coat with a wire-pin brush, making absolutely sure it is one with rounded tips. Check to see if the feet need trimming, i.e. the hair that grows between the pads, and then let the dog out to relieve itself – let's hope it's not pouring with rain!

When you get to a show, hopefully the dog will still be fairly clean, but nonetheless you will need to attend to its coat. Use a light grooming spray and go through the coat and fringes with a brush and then a comb, and make sure that the eyes are clean. We usually freshen up a dog by using a damp pad of cotton-wool (cotton) and wiping its face. Make sure the feet and the front leg fringes are clean. If your dog looks grubby, apply some self-rinse shampoo and towel off. Apply a little talcum powder/corn starch, leave to dry for about ten minutes, and then brush through the coat. Before you go into the ring, make sure that all the powder has been brushed out. The males are the worst, as they always seem to be lifting their legs, and getting their nice clean coat wet, and sometimes stained. We spray the under part of the dog with some self-rinse shampoo, towel off, and then apply some talcum powder/corn starch. As above, leave to dry for about ten minutes and then brush through the coat.

Check the dog again about twenty minutes before it is due in the ring; you could possibly apply a little talcum powder to the under part, and then brush it out. About five minutes before you are due in the ring, get the dog out, check its coat again, fasten the show lead (making sure you do not catch any ear fringes in the lead) and off you go!

SHOW GROOMING KIT

Bristle brush
Wire-pin brush (with rounded tips)
Double-ended comb
Talcum powder/corn starch
Cotton pads
Self-rinse shampoo
Anti-static coat spray
Towel.

# Chapter Five

# TRAINING

Basic training and good manners should be taught to all dogs, no matter how big or how small, so that they are a pleasure to own and to know in all situations. There is no point in having a badly behaved dog who has to be shut away in another room whenever you have visitors to the house. If your dog is well behaved you will have plenty of invitations to other people's houses and other social events. Some owners worry that imposing this sort of discipline on a dog will mean that it will lose its sense of fun and mischief, but this is not the case; it simply means that you establish who is master, and your dog understands the rules it must live by.

Training can never start too early, provided, that is, that the lessons are short and enjoyable for both dog and owner. The first lesson a puppy must learn is the word 'No'. It is important not to confuse the puppy with lots of different words, but to restrict yourself to a simple 'No' when the puppy is doing something wrong, such as chewing your slipper or shoe, or trying to teethe on your finger. When you have said 'No', try and distract the puppy from what it is doing by giving it one of its own toys that it is allowed to chew. As part of its early training a puppy should become accustomed to various noises such as the vacuum cleaner, the washing machine, the radio – all sorts of things that are commonplace to us, but could easily frighten a young puppy.

The pup should also get used to having visitors in the house; some puppies will bound up to all and sundry, but others are hesitant and not quite so sure of themselves. Never tell a puppy off if it is being shy or withdrawn, because this will not help the situation at all. The best policy in this situation is to ignore the puppy, and sometimes curiosity will get the better of it, and it will come out and have a look at the visitor. Do not try and grab the puppy, but talk reassuringly to it and gently encourage it to come forward and meet the stranger. It may help if you let the

*Shevarl Skippers Son, pictured at five months. Training can never start too early, and the sooner your puppy learns to respond to you, the better.*

puppy sit on your lap, and then let the visitor talk to it and make a fuss of it. Do not try and force the situation; the puppy will come round in its own good time. If you have an excitable puppy, make sure it is on the floor when it is introduced to visitors, and ask the visitor to sit on the floor when making a fuss of the puppy. Papillons are so quick, and sometimes they seem to almost fly out of your arms. Consequently, it is very easy for accidents to happen, as a Pap could land badly on the floor. A lot of people are in the habit of picking up their Papillon when someone comes to the house, but although this may seem harmless enough, it could lead to problems. The dog may become protective towards you, and may try to 'guard' you when someone approaches. At worst, this could result in the dog snapping, which is the sort of anti-social behaviour that no dog owner should tolerate. Most dogs will try and push their luck just to see how far you will let them go – they are very like children in this way – so you must be sensible and use your commonsense at all times.

As soon as the puppy has had its vaccinations it is ready to explore the outside world, and this is full of strange noises and experiences such as traffic going by, people and children out walking, dogs, cats, dustbins to walk past – there is no end to the distractions in a busy street. Some puppies take all this in their stride, others tend to be more timid, and you will need to encourage and reassure the puppy all the time. Obviously it helps if the puppy is used to walking on a lead, and this can be practised in the garden before it has completed its vaccinations. It is also a good idea to teach the puppy to come to you when it is called by name. Most puppies pick this up very quickly, especially if they are rewarded with plenty of praise and a tasty titbit. Nearly all towns have a dog training club, and it is well worth taking your puppy along, even if you are only hoping to achieve basic obedience with it. Most reputable clubs will ask to see the dog's vaccination certificate before they can accept it into the class. If you enrol on a training course it is important to remember that practice at home is essential. You will make no progress if you do the exercises in the class and then forget all about them until the next week. Practise every day for five to ten minutes at a time, and always try and finish up when the dog has done something well and you give plenty of praise. In this way the puppy will look forward to its next lesson. When you are training, do not give your dog lots of commands, for instance: "Sit, sit Scamp, come Scamp,sit down, sit, I've told you sit ..." This will completely confuse the dog. All that is required is to attract the dog's attention by using its name, and then give the command "Scamp, sit". The basic requirement for pet obedience is to walk to heel on and off the lead, to do a recall, i.e. to come when called, to go into the down position and to stand. There are several different methods of teaching dogs these exercises, so it is best to be guided by a good instructor. Papillons like to have something to occupy their minds, and so most will respond well to training classes. Play can also be used as a form of training. For instance, if you throw a ball or toy and the dog brings it back to you, call its name, and you are then on your way to doing a recall. You can take this one step further by making the dog sit when you throw the ball, and then let him bring it back to you. A tug of war can sometimes be fun, but you must not let the dog win every time, otherwise it will start to think that it is dominant and the leader of the pack. All dogs, even toy dogs, are pack animals and they must learn that the human is the leader of the pack.

Some Papillon owners take training a stage further and enter obedience competitions and go in for agility contests. This can be great fun, but it is very time-consuming, and endless patience is required for both disciplines. In Britain Mrs Radermacher blazed a trail for Papillons in the Obedience ring with Marquita Of Harleymeads, who achieved considerable success before the Second World War. Mrs A. Foreman is well-known for her obedience work with Papillons, which she has specialised in for many years. She gives demonstrations of her dogs working, which we found absolutely fascinating to watch. We saw her Papillons doing heel work, sit, stay and retrieving an object. In this case it was a long plastic sword, which the Papillon proudly carried back to Mrs Foreman, tail wagging and loving every minute of it. The finale was a Papillon pulling a toy lorry with another Papillon sitting in it. They made it look so easy, but this sort of thing takes a great deal of hard work and training. Mrs Foreman also exhibits in the show ring with great success, and she has bred Champions which also carry the Companion Dog Excellent (CDEX) title, proving that Papillons have both brains and beauty. Two of her best-known dogs are Bordercott Sock, a CC winner who was trained up to Test C in Obedience, and Ch. Ember Of Bordercott, who won Best of Breed at Crufts and was also a first prize winner in Obedience competitions. Agility is now very popular, and not only with such breeds as Border Collies and German Shepherds; Papillons are also taking part and proving very successful. Eleanor Thomas and her Papillon Danica Fuchsia, known to her friends as 'Tikki', have put the breed on the map, winning a number of competitions, including the Pedigree Chum Mini Agility Finals at the Olympia International Show-jumping Championships, the most prestigious of all the agility events, and Tikki was the smallest and the youngest dog to compete. Eleanor's other dog, Minky, who is nine and half inches tall, won

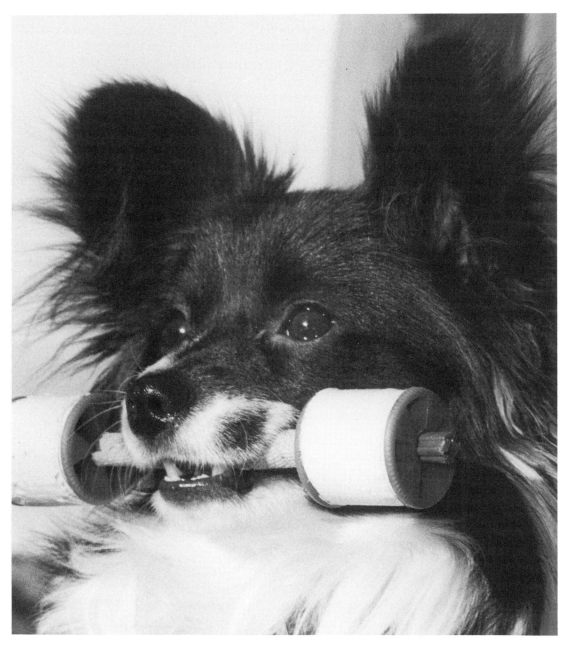

*Lordsrake Moffat, pictured at ten months. The Papillon is an intelligent breed, and a number have been trained to compete successfully in Obedience competitions.*

the first ever Bonio All-round Mini Agility Dog Of The Year contest, competing against fifty-eight other dogs. The standard in mini agility rises every year, and there are now some ninety dogs who compete for just six rosettes. Competition is obviously very intense, but the dogs clearly love every minute of it. They are certainly a joy to watch, and a mighty cheer goes up as they clear the obstacles. Obedience is taken very seriously in the U.S.A., and many Papillon owners are now competing in this field, proving how intelligent and versatile the breed can be.

# Chapter Six

# THE BREED STANDARD

The Breed Standard is the blueprint for the breed. Breeders should aim to breed as true to the standard as they can, and judges must use it as their bible when assessing the breed in the show ring. With a coated breed like the Papillon you have to get your hands on the dog, as the coat can hide a lot of good and bad points. For instance, the dog can appear to have a good body, but maybe under all that coat it is slab-sided, or its elbows may stick out. With a wealth of coat, the topline can look a little suspect, but again, it is only when you go over the dog and see exactly what is under the coat, that you can make an accurate judgement. It is important to bear in mind that beauty is in the eye of the beholder, so not all judges will agree with each other; and that is what makes breeding and showing such a challenge. The perfect dog is yet to be born, and we are all striving to improve. If you ever think you have the perfect dog in your kennel, then it is time to give up!

The Breed Standards that are used in Britain and America are similar in all their essential points, with a few minor differences which we have highlighted in our analysis. The American Breed Standard was updated in 1991. On the continent the Federation Cynologique Internationale (FCI) Standard is used, and this is far more detailed than either the American or the British versions, and it differs in a number of breed points. However, we think it is important to contrast the three Breed Standards in order to form a complete picture, for after all, the Papillon is descended from the continental Toy Spaniel.

## THE BRITISH BREED STANDARD

GENERAL APPEARANCE Dainty, well balanced little dog. An alert bearing and intelligent expression.

CHARACTERISTICS The name 'Papillon' is derived from the shape and position of the ears. When erect they are carried obliquely like the spread wings of the butterfly, hence the name. When the ears are completely dropped this type is known as the Phalene (Moth). Head markings should be symmetrical, about a narrow white clearly defined blaze which is desirable but not essential to represent the body of a butterfly.

TEMPERAMENT Lively, intelligent, friendly with no aggression; always alert.

HEAD AND SKULL Skull slightly rounded between ears, muzzle finely pointed and abruptly finer than the skull, accentuating well-defined stop, length from tip of nose to stop approximately a third the length of head. Nose black.

EYES Medium size, rounded, never bulging, dark with dark rims placed rather low in the skull.

EARS Very large, mobile with rounded tips, heavily fringed; set towards back of head, far enough apart to show the slightly rounded shape of skull. Leathers firm but fine. When erect each ear should form an angle of approximately 45 degrees to head.

MOUTH Jaws strong, with perfect, regular and complete scissor bite, i.e. the upper teeth closely overlapping the lower teeth and set square to the jaws. Lips thin, tight and dark in colour.

NECK Medium length.

FOREQUARTERS Shoulders well developed and sloping. Chest rather deep. Forelegs straight, slender and fine-boned. Elbows close to chest.

BODY Fairly long with level topline; well sprung ribs, loin strong, of good length slightly arched belly.

HINDQUARTERS Well developed, well turned stifle. Legs when viewed from behind parallel. Dewclaws on hindlegs removed.

FEET Fairly long, hare-like, tufts of hair between toes extending far beyond them.

TAIL Long, well fringed, set on high, arched over back with fringes falling to side to form a plume.

GAIT/MOVEMENT Light, free-flowing, positive and free from any restriction. Viewed from in front or behind, legs and feet moving parallel to each other, with feet turning neither in nor out. Viewed from side dog covering ground well with no hint of hackneyed action.

COAT Abundant, flowing but without undercoat; long, fine, silky, falling flat on back and sides; profuse frill on chest; short and close on skull, muzzle and front parts of legs. Rear of forelegs to pasterns, tail and thighs covered with long hair.

COLOUR White with patches, which may be any colour except liver. Tricolours black and white with tan spots over eyes, tan inside ears on cheeks, and under root of tail.

SIZE Height: 20-28cms. (8-11 ins.). Dog will appear slightly longer than high when properly furnished with ruff and hind fringes.

FAULTS Any departure from the foregoing points should be considered a fault and the seriousness with which the fault should be regarded should be in exact proportion to the degree.

NOTE Male animals should have two apparently normal testicles fully descended into the scrotum.

*Reproduced by kind permission of the English Kennel Club.*

## THE AMERICAN BREED STANDARD

GENERAL APPEARANCE The Papillon is a small, friendly, elegant toy dog of fine-boned structure, light, dainty and of lively action; distinguished from other breeds by its beautiful butterfly-like ears.

SIZE PROPORTION, SUBSTANCE
Size – Height at withers, 8 to 11 inches. Fault – Over 11 inches. Disqualifcation – Over 12 inches.
Proportion – Body must be slightly longer than the height at withers. It is not a cobby dog. Weight is in proportion to height.
Substance – Of fine-boned structure.

*Ch. Daneview Charleston: a typical Papillon, with profuse feathering.*

HEAD
Eyes  dark, round, not bulging, of medium size and alert in expression. The inner corners of the eyes are on line with the stop. Eye rims black.
Ears – The ears of either the erect or drop type should be large with rounded tips, and set on the sides and toward the back of the head.
(1) Ears of the erect type are carried obliquely and move like the spread wings of a butterfly. When alert, each ear forms an angle of approximately 45 degrees to the head. The leather should be of sufficient strength to maintain the erect position.
(2) Ears of the drop type, known as the Phalene, are similar to the erect type, but are carried drooping and must be completely down. Faults – Ears small, pointed, set too high; one ear up, or ears partly down.

*Noveau Little Meggy: a solid-headed black and white Papillon, proving that the solid head, which is permitted in the Breed Standard, does not detract from the breed's lovely expression.*

*Pierosas Albertina At Tussalud: The Phalene has the same Breed Standard as the Papillon, with the exception of the drop ears.*

Skull – The head is small. The skull is of medium width and slightly rounded between the ears. A well-defined stop is formed where the muzzle joins the skull.

Muzzle – The muzzle is fine, abruptly thinner than the head, tapering to the nose. The length of the muzzle from the tip of the nose to stop is approximately one-third the length of the head from tip of nose to occiput.

Nose black, small, rounded and slightly flat on top.

The following faults shall be severely penalized – Nose not black.

Lips tight, thin and black. Tongue must not be visible when jaws are closed.

Bite – Teeth must meet in a scissors bite.

Faults—Overshot or undershot.

NECK TOPLINE AND BODY

Neck of medium length.

Topline – The backline is straight and level.

Body – The chest is of medium depth with ribs well sprung. The belly is tucked up.

Tail long, set high and carried well arched over the body. The tail is covered with a long, flowing plume. The plume may hang to either side of the body.

Faults – Low-set tail; one not arched over the back, or too short.

FOREQUARTERS Shoulders well developed and laid back to allow freedom of movement. Forelegs slender, fine-boned and must be straight. Removal of dewclaws on forelegs optional. Front feet thin and elongated (hare-like), pointing neither in nor out.

HINDQUARTERS Well developed and well angulated. The hind legs are slender, fine-boned, and parallel when viewed from behind. Hocks inclined neither in nor out. Dewclaws, if any, must be removed from hind legs. Hind feet thin and elongated (hare-like), pointing neither in nor out.

COAT Abundant, long, fine, silky, flowing, straight with resilient quality, flat on back and sides of body. A profuse frill on chest. There is no undercoat. Hair short and close on skull, muzzle, front of forelegs, and from hind feet to hocks. Ears well fringed, with the inside covered with silken hair of medium length. Backs of the forelegs are covered with feathers diminishing to the pasterns. Hind legs are covered to the hocks with abundant breeches (culottes). Tail is covered with a long, flowing plume. Hair on feet is short, but fine tufts may appear over toes and grow beyond them, forming a point.

COLOR Always parti-color or white with patches of any color(s). On the head, color(s) other than white must cover both ears, back and front, and extend without interruption from the ears over both eyes. A clearly defined white blaze and noseband are preferred to a solidly marked head. Symmetry of facial markings is desirable. The size, shape, placement, and presence or absence of patches of color on the body are without importance. Among the colors there is no preference, provided nose, eye rims and lips are well pigmented black.

The following faults shall be severely penalized – Color other than white not covering both ears, back and front, or not extending from the ears over both eyes. A slight extension of the white collar onto the base of the ears, or a few white hairs interspersed among the color, shall not be penalized, provided the butterfly appearance is not sacrificed.

Disqualifications – An all white dog or a dog with no white.

GAIT Free, quick, easy, graceful, not paddle-footed, or stiff in hip movements.

TEMPERAMENT Happy, alert and fnendly. Neither shy nor aggressive.

DISQUALIFICATIONS Height over 12 inches. An all white dog or a dog with no white.

*Approved June 10, 1991*

*Reproduced by kind permission of the American Kennel Club.*

## THE FCI STANDARD

GENERAL APPEARANCE The Continental Toy Spaniel is a tiny 'edition de luxe' Spaniel of normal and harmonious structure, with a profuse coat, moderate length of muzzle (it is shorter than the skull), graceful but nevertheless smart appearance, displaying a proud carriage and a free elegant action. The body is slightly longer than high.

HEAD The different parts are well proportioned to each other, the head as a whole being comparatively lighter and shorter than the one of tall and middle size Spaniels. Seen from the front and from the side the skull appears slightly rounded between the ears; it sometimes shows a hint of a groove. The muzzle is shorter than the skull, fine and tapering towards the nose but without too much lateral flattening: it should by no means be upturned. The bridge of the nose is straight and forms a well defined stop with the forehead. Heavier dogs have a less marked stop whereas the latter is clearly defined on very small dogs, although it should never be too square.

NOSE Small, black and rounded, slightly flat on top.

LIPS Strongly pigmented, thin and tight.

TEETH Rather strong; even and normal bite.

TONGUE The tongue should not be visible. The fact that it remains permanently visible or does not disappear when touched with the finger is a disqualifying fault.

EYES Quite large, well opened, of very broad almond shape, not bulging and rather low set, this is on a line with the stop. They should be dark and expressive, with well pigmented lids.

EARS They should be of fine leather but of sufficient strength to maintain the opened-up position. In the erect as well as in the drop type the supporting cartilage should not finish in an exaggeratedly pointed tip (to be checked by feeling with the hand). The ears are set rather backwards and sufficiently wide apart to disclose the slightly rounded forehead.
a) The drop type (Phalene).
At rest they are high set, fairly above the eye line; they are carried drooping but are nevertheless quite mobile. They are covered with wavy hair that can be very long and is contributing to the cute look of the dog.
b) The erect type (Papillon).
The ears are high set with a largely opened concha, carried obliquely, forming an angle of approximately 45 degrees to the head. The ears should by no means point upwards and resemble those of the Spitz; This latter feature should be severely penalized. The inside of the concha is covered with silky, wavy hair that reaches slightly over the rim; the outer side is covered with long, wavy fringes that reach far over the rim of the ears. A crossing between the two types often results in ears that are partly drooping, that is with the tips hanging over; this intermediate ear carriage is a severe fault.

SHOULDERS The scapula and humerus are well developed and of identical length; they form a normal angle and firmly set.

FORE AND REAR LEGS Straight, rather fine. The dog must not appear leggy. Seen from the side, the carpus is almost invisible; the hocks are normally bent; all four legs are parallel when viewed from the front as from the rear.

FEET The feet should be elongated (hare-like) and well resting on the soles. The nails are strong and, ideally, of black colour; brown and white dogs may have slightly lighter coloured nails (white nails are not considered a fault with all-white dogs and with those having white feet as long as the general pigmentation is correct). The toes are thin and well padded; tufts of thin, long hair might appear between the toes and grow beyond them forming a point.

NECK Of medium length with a slightly bent crest.

BODY

Chest: Wide and deep. The girth, measured between the two last ribs, should more or less equal the height at the withers.   The ribs are well sprung.

Topline: Neither too short, nor arched or hollow; loins strong and slightly arched.

Belly: Slightly tucked up.

TAIL Set high, rather long, with long feathering forming a lovely plume. When the dog is attentive, the tail is carried well arched over the body; the tip may slightly touch the back; the tail should never be curled or carried flat on the back.

COAT The coat is profuse, shiny and wavy (not curly); no undercoat. The hair in itself is not limp but rather somewhat resilient, with a silken look. The hair is flat and comparatively fine, slightly bent. On the whole it reminds you of the coat of the small English Spaniels but is quite different from that of the Pekingese; on the other hand, it should by no means resemble the coat of the Spitz. The hair is short and smooth on the head, the front of the legs and on the back of legs from the hocks downward; on the body it is of medium length getting longer towards the neck where it forms a frill that is gracefully flowing over the breast. The ears and the rearside of the forelegs are feathered; the rear of the thighs is covered with abundant breeches. Fine tufts of hair may appear between the toes as long as they do not make the feet look clumsy but on the contrary give it an even more refined and elongated appearance. The hair of some dogs with a very profuse coat has a length of 7.5cms. on the withers, the feathering of the tail reaching some 15cm.

COLOURS Any colour permitted. All dogs, even the pure white ones must have well pigmented lips and eye rims and most of all black noses.

HEIGHT The maximum height at the withers is 28cms.

WEIGHT Minimum weight: 1.500kg.
There are two varieties:
1  Under 2.5kg. for males and bitches.
2. From 2.5kg. to 4.5kg. for males, from 2.5 to 5 kg. for bitches.

LENGTH OF BODY This is to be measured from the point of the shoulder to the far end of the ischium.

HEIGHT To be measured at the withers.

GAIT Proud. Free, easy, graceful.

FAULTS Flat skull, 'apple head' or domed skull similar to that of English Toy Spaniels. Too sharply or insufficiently marked stop. Convex or concave nosebridge. Small, protruding, too roundish and light eyes; visible white when the eyes are looking straight forward. Any other colour of the nose than black. Pink spots on lids and lips. Over and (worse) undershot mouths are to be avoided. Crooked forelegs; marked (knotlike) carpus; any position of the rear legs that is deviating from the regular parallel stand from the stifles downwards, feet included. Weak rear. Out or in-turned feet; nails not touching the ground; single or double dewclaws at the hind legs are undesirable and considered a blemish regarding the beauty of the dog; they should therefore be removed. A curled tail or a tail carried flat along the spine, or hanging sideways. It should be noted that this means the tail itself, not the feathering which, due to its length, is hanging in tufts.

A thin, soft or blown-up, off-standing coat; straight hair; woolly coat; undercoat betraying a cross with the Spitz. A roach or sway back.

DISQUALIFICATION

1. A pink nose or one having pink spots.
2. Marked over or undershot mouth (the upper and lower incisors not touching each other).
3. Paralysed or permanently visible tongue.

*Reproduced by kind permission of the Federation Cynologique Internationale.*

## ANALYSIS OF THE BREED STANDARD

### GENERAL APPEARANCE

This is described well in all three Breed Standards. The Papillon must look, and be, dainty. It must not have coarse or thick bone, or this will make the dog look coarse and cloddy. The Papillon is named after a butterfly, and this should be reflected in its overall dainty appearance. It should always be well balanced in structure, and when the Papillon is in full coat it should 'appear' to be slightly longer than it is high. This is achieved because the ruff and the trousers give added length to the body, but underneath this wealth of coat the Papillon is basically square. It should have an alert and intelligent expression, which is one of the characteristics of the breed, and one of its particular attractions.

### CHARACTERISTICS

The English Breed Standard covers this in a separate heading, but most of the points are covered in the General Appearance descriptions in the American and FCI Standards. The English wording regarding the ears: "When erect they are carried obliquely like the spread wings of a butterfly", is an excellent description, and when fully fringed, the ears do look absolutely beautiful. The Phalenes are not particularly numerous in Britain; however, great attention should be given to correct ear placement. This variety should carry its ears in a dropped position – like a moth, rather than a butterfly. Head markings should be symmetrical; a narrow white clearly defined blaze is desirable, but not essential. This is an important point to bear in mind, particularly when judging the breed. Obviously, a Papillon with a perfect blaze is to be aimed for, but, as we all know, nature does not produce perfect specimens. Expression is far more important than a plain head with a perfect blaze. The head must always retain that alert and pretty expression that we expect from a Papillon, but if the blaze is not perfect, it is not the end of the world. There have been Champions made up without blazes – and these are described as having a 'solid head'.

*Correct type*

*Incorrect type: ears are set too upright and are pointed, the topline dips from the shoulders to the withers, and the tail is flat on the back.*

## TEMPERAMENT

Again, the English Breed Standard is the only one to cover this under a separate heading. The Papillon seems to fly around a bit like a butterfly and is always inquisitive, so 'lively' and 'alert' are apt descriptions. They are certainly intelligent, and this is one of the charms of this breed. There is no place for aggression, and Papillons should be outgoing and friendly.

## HEAD

The head is an important part of the Papillon, as this is what makes it different from other breeds. Under this heading, the American Breed Standard starts with 'Small', as used to be the case in the British version. Unfortunately, the word 'small' has now been discarded, and we think this is a great shame. A large head, or one that is out of proportion to the body, would detract from the general daintiness that is required. The old English Standard stated: "Head and skull small and characteristically proportionate to the body", and we believe this was a valuable description, and the Standard is poorer without it.

The head should be slightly rounded between the ears: we do not want an apple-domed head, neither do we want a flat skull. The muzzle should be finely pointed; nothing looks worse than a round, thick or coarse muzzle, as it detracts from the daintiness of the breed. Equally, the muzzle should not be so thin as to appear weak. The ideal is a muzzle that is abruptly finer than the skull and finely pointed, which will accentuate the well-defined stop. We do not want a sloping stop, but a definite stop which tells us where the nose starts from. The nose is approximately one-third the length of the head; the skull makes up the other two-thirds. If you have too short a nose it can give the appearance of a Chihuahua's head, which is not desirable. However, you do not want a nose that is too long, as this would also spoil the balance of the head and the expression, making the dog look snipey. The nose must always be black; there is simply no other colour other than black and the whole of the nose must be black – a spotted nose is not acceptable. In America a nose that is not black is severely penalised, and under FCI a pink nose or a nose with pink spots counts as a disqualification. The AKC and the FCI are more explicit about the shape of the nose, calling for it to be small, rounded and slightly flat on top.

## EYES

These should be of medium size and rounded, dark in colour and with dark eye-rims, placed rather low in the skull so that the corners of eye are basically level with the stop. The eyes should not be too close together or too small, as this would give a mean or 'piggy' expression, whereas the bright, alert expression is an integral characteristic of the breed. The AKC requires black eye-rims, rather than 'dark' or 'well pigmented' as described in the other two Standards. The FCI also differs in its description of shape, stating 'very broad, almond-shape'. However, all three versions agree that the eyes should never be bulging.

## EARS

The ears are another very important feature of the breed, and make it look different from all other toy breeds. The ears are very large and mobile, with rounded tips – never pointed or triangular. They should be heavily fringed – this usually comes with maturity – and they should be set towards the back of the head and far enough apart for the slightly rounded shape of the skull to be seen. When erect, each ear should form an angle of approximately 45 degrees to the head. The ear placement is all-important. If the ears are set too high on top of the head, you cannot see the rounded shape of the skull, and this spoils the appearance of the head; if they are set too low and come out of the side of the head, this also destroys the overall balance of the head. If you envisage the silhouette of a butterfly, this gives you the most accurate idea of correct shape and position of the ears. The leathers (the actual ear itself) should be firm – this means the ear should be erect – but they should be fine, as thick ear leathers could result in an appearance of coarseness. All three Breed Standards are very similar in their descriptions of this feature, except that the AKC and the FCI versions go into detail about the Phalene ears.

MOUTH
All three Breed Standards ask for a complete scissor bite. Overshot and undershot mouths are disqualifying faults under FCI rules. The AKC requires black lips, rather than the 'dark' or

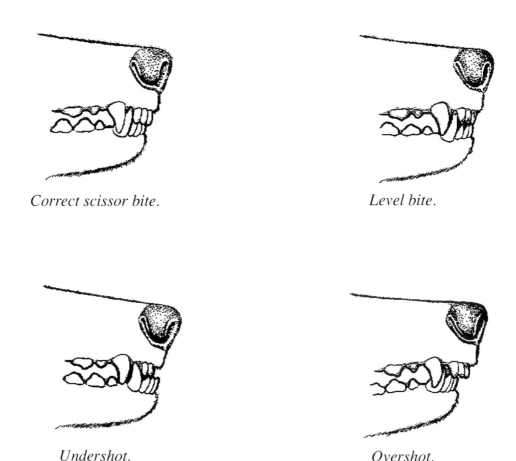

*Correct scissor bite.*                                    *Level bite.*


*Undershot.*                                              *Overshot.*

'strongly pigmented' asked for in the other two Standards. The tongue is also mentioned in the FCI Standard, specifying that it should not be visible. It is a disqualifying fault if the tongue remains permanently visible, or if it is not retracted when it is touched with a finger.

NECK

If the neck is of a medium length, this helps to give the dog an overall balance, and a proud head carriage. A neck that is short and stuffy does not enhance a Papillon.

FOREQUARTERS

The shoulders should be well developed and sloping. If a dog has an upright shoulder, it often seems to go with a short and stuffy neck, it also results in a restricted movement – rather than the dog moving with a good reach, it takes lots of short steps to cover the ground. If the shoulders are set at an angle of 45 degrees, this usually goes with a good reach of neck. This not only helps with the overall outline of the dog, but also enables the dog to reach out over the ground, as required. The chest should be rather deep; a shallow or flat chest is undesirable. The forelegs

*Correct.*

*Toeing in.*

*Too narrow.*

*Toeing out.*

*Bowed.*

should be straight, slender and fine-boned – and this is vital. The bone must be sound, of quality, and straight, and the elbows must be close to the chest. It is very unsightly when a Papillon has elbows that stick out.

BODY

A level topline is most important. A roached topline, or a topline that dips at the withers, should be severely penalised. The body must be of good length. Basically, the measurement from the withers to the ground and from the withers to the tail should be the same. If the body is too short it will resemble a Pomeranian. The American Standard states that a Papillon must be slightly longer than the height at the withers, and that it is not a cobby dog (i.e. short-coupled). The British Standard calls for the body to be fairly long, but under the description for size it states: 'Dogs will appear slightly longer than high when properly furnished with ruff and hind fringes.'

HINDQUARTERS

If an animal is to move with 'drive', it is essential that it should have a good turn of stifle. Legs

*Correct.*

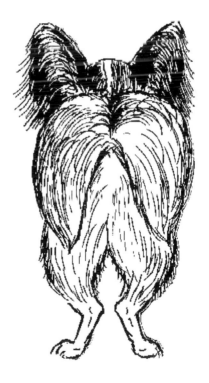

*Cow hocks.*

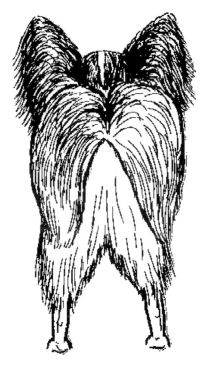

*Too wide.*

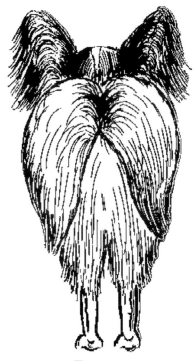

*Too narrow.*

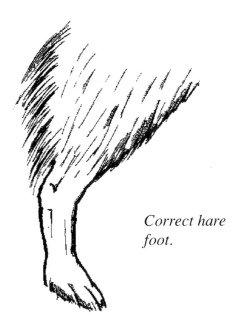

*Correct hare foot.*

when viewed from behind should be parallel with the feet, turning neither in nor out. When moving away, they should move true and straight, with drive. A Papillon might be a toy breed, but that is no reason why it should not be well muscled, like its 'sporting' cousins.

FEET

These are another important feature of the breed. Round cat-like feet should be penalised, as this would spoil the daintiness of this fine-boned dog. The hare foot is slender and slightly long. Tufts of hair extending far beyond the toes – this is self explanatory, and the toe fringes are much prized. The nails merit a detailed description in the FCI Standard.

## TAIL

The tail should be long and set on high, so it is carried well over the back and not flat to the back. It should be arched over the back to enhance the outline, and when the long tail feathers of a mature dog cascade down, a plume is created, arched above the level of the back.

## GAIT/MOVEMENT

As the Papillon is a dainty dog, the movement should be light and free-flowing. You would not want a dog that is stomping along, looking as if walking was a real effort. The legs should be placed positively on the ground as it moves along, but without any restriction. This means that the joints and muscles that move the legs should be like a well-oiled machine, moving effortlessly. There should be no exaggerated movements, i.e. no hackney action, which is definitely not free and flowing movement. Legs and feet should move parallel to each other, with feet turning neither in nor out. It is very unsightly when a dog stands with its feet turning out at ten-to-two, or for that matter, with its feet turning in. This fault often goes with a bowed or wide front or rear. When the dog is viewed from the side, it should cover the ground well. It is a

*Correct gait.*

*Incorrect gait: showing upright shoulders, which will not allow full extension, thus creating 'daisy-clipping' or restricted movement.*

lovely sight when a Papillon is on the move, just 'flowing' around the ring, and covering the ground well, despite its small size.

## COAT

A coat of the correct texture is highly desirable. It should be abundant and flowing, but without any undercoat. A stand-off or fluffy coat should be faulted. The dog should have a profuse frill on its chest, and the tail and thigh should be covered in long hair. However, short and close hair is required on muzzle, skull and the front of legs. Do not be side-tracked by the word 'abundant'. The texture is also important, as is the 'lie' of the coat. If the coat is of the correct texture, i.e. flowing and silky, as against fluffy, stand-off or woolly, then no trimming should be required. The FCI Standard asks for a coat that is profuse, shiny and wavy (not curly). The hair should be flat and comparatively fine.

## COLOUR

The predominant colour is white, with patches of any colour, bar liver. This is because a liver coat-colour always goes with a liver-coloured nose, which is prohibited in the Breed Standard. There is a wide variety of colours: from a pale lemon to coal black, all shades of sable, such as red sable, fawn sable, pure red and tri-colour. In the American Standard an all-white dog, or a dog with no white colouring would be disqualified. The FCI permits all colours – even those that are pure white, so long as the nose is black and the lips and eye rims are well pigmented. There is no reference to symmetrical head markings, and therefore solid heads of any colour are permissible.

SIZE

In a toy breed the difference between 8 and 11 inches, as stipulated in the British and American Standards, is considerable. If you stand an 8 inch dog next to an 11 inch dog, you are aware of a very marked contrast in size. However, both are correct. In America dogs over 11 inches are faulted,and dogs over 12 inches are disqualified. Most breeders try and aim for a happy medium between the 8 inch and 11 inch extremes, but it is not inches, it is the overall daintiness of the dog that is of paramount importance. In the old British Standard there was an ideal weight: Adult dogs 3lbs to 5lbs; adult bitches from 4lbs to 7 lbs. The FCI stipulates a minimum weight of 1.500kg., and then specifies two weights for different varieties: under 2.5kg. for males and bitches, and from 2.5kg. to 4.5kg. for bitches and from 2.5kg. to 5kg. for males, with a maximum height at the withers of 28cm (i.e. 11 inches).

Despite the superficial differences, we think that, at the end of the day, both the American Kennel Club and the English Kennel Club have very similar ideas on the Papillon Breed Standard. There are more marked differences with the FCI Standard. However, there will always be some points in every Breed Standard that are not exactly crystal clear, and these remain open to interpretation. It is therefore the duty of all breeders and judges to keep the future welfare of the breed in mind so that we have typical-looking Papillons that are sound in body and mind.

68

# Chapter Seven

# THE SHOW RING

Showing a Papillon can be a very interesting hobby, not only for the chance of competing with your dog, but because it also gives you the opportunity to visit different parts of the country and it is a place to meet and make friends, and it can be a most enjoyable day out. One thing to remember is that at the end of the day you take the same dog home with you, whether it has won a first prize or not; so, win or lose, you have still got your lovely Papillon.

Training for the show ring can never start too early. Whether it is socialising your puppy or getting it used to being handled and training it to stand on the table, the sooner it gets used to routine, the better. Never overdo things with a young puppy, it is far more beneficial to work with a puppy for a couple of minutes, three or four times a day, than to attempt a fifteen minute session all in one go. Puppies get bored very easily, so try to make show training fun, so that the puppy looks forward to it and enjoys it. We start socialising our puppies from the moment they are born, picking them up and talking to them. By the time they are three weeks old and weaning has started, the puppies become quite people-conscious. At about four weeks they start to play with their littermates, and you can introduce a few safe toys to stimulate play. When the litter is five weeks old we take each puppy and stand it on a non-slip surface for about thirty seconds, giving plenty of encouragement and reassurance. Make sure you keep hold of the puppy, in case it should fall or try to jump off the table. This is the first stage in training your puppy to stand on the table for the judge to 'go over the dog'. Practise this a couple of times a day, and gradually you can start to position the puppy's legs so that it stands four square. The next stage is to go over the puppy as a judge would, but this must be done very gently and with plenty of praise and encouragement. The pup may be rather sensitive about having its teeth looked at, especially if it is teething, so you must be particularly careful in this area.

In the show ring it is important that the dog looks alert and interested, and so the next step is to get the puppy to pay attention to you, and to listen to you. We achieve this by putting some food in a crackly paper bag; the bag is used to get the puppy's attention, and then it is rewarded with a small piece of meat. We usually do this in the kitchen when the puppy is running around or playing. Call the puppy by name to attract its attention, and then give the command "stand". Then, talk to the puppy, rustling the bag for a very short time to start with, and then immediately reward it with a piece of meat. Do not give the titbit if the puppy does not do what you want it to. Try this routine three or four times, and then put the bag away and try the exercise using the command "stand" and rewarding with a titbit. Again, this training should take place in very short spells.

Next comes lead training. Some Papillons take to this like a duck to water, others protest most strongly! We use a light show lead, and carry the puppy from the house to a part of the garden that it is not familiar with. Put the puppy down, and just follow the puppy on the lead wherever it wants to go. When it is moving forward confidently try and coax the puppy to follow you. As soon as it does this, give plenty of praise and end the lesson. Always try and end a lesson when the puppy has done something right. Do not be tempted to push on a bit further – there is always tomorrow for the next lesson. The three basics to concentrate on are table training, paying attention and standing, and lead training. As the lead training progresses you can teach the puppy to walk up and down in straight line. You can then progress to walking in a triangle and getting the puppy to stand on the lead, rewarding it with a titbit, just as you have been doing in the kitchen.

When you have gained the puppy's confidence, and it has had all its vaccinations, it is a good idea to take it to ringcraft classes, which are designed specially for show dogs. However, be careful, as you do not want to undo all the good work you have already done by rushing things now. Watch out for how your dog reacts when you get to the class, and if it is a little apprehensive, let it sit in the travelling box and watch what is going on. When the puppy has had a chance to get used to all the noise, bring it out of its box and let it sit somewhere quietly, so it can gain some confidence. If you really think the pup is ready to join the class, try and get beside a small and well behaved dog. This sounds as if we are advocating that you should be over-protective with your dog, but if you put your puppy off at this stage it will take a long time to regain its confidence. When it is your turn, put the puppy on the non-slip surface of the table, standing up so that it is ready for the handler's examination. Talk to your puppy all the time, reassuring it and telling it how clever it is. After the examination you will be asked to move the puppy up and down. Place the dog on the floor, make sure its lead is in position, and then off you go, talking to it and encouraging it so that you transfer a feeling of enjoyment. When you get back to the handler, command the puppy to "stand", and then reward with a titbit. On the first occasion do not give your puppy too much to do, it will be sufficient if it completes all the exercises once only, as it is a lot for a young puppy to absorb. Ringcraft class can be of great benefit to both you and the puppy. If you are a newcomer to the show world it can give you a good grounding as to what is expected in the ring, and it is of immense value to the puppy as it will get used to being handled by different people, meeting other dogs both large and small, travelling in a car, and all the different noises and smells. Some clubs hold competitions or matches, which can be good fun and give you a taste of competition before you try your luck in the show ring.

There are six types of shows in Britain and they are Matches, Exemption Shows, Sanction Shows, Limit Shows, Open Shows and Championship Shows, and details are always advertised in the canine Press.When you apply for an entry form you will be sent a schedule where all the rules and regulations are explained. On the entry form you will need to fill in the registered name of the dog, its date of birth, the sire and the dam and the number of the class that you are entering. The basic classes are: Minor puppy for dogs of between six and nine months of age, Puppy for dogs of six to twelve months old, Junior for dogs of six to eighteen months old, Novice, Post Graduate and Limit, which are all dependent on the number of first prizes your dog has won, and the Open class is open to all dogs and bitches. The most important and prestigious shows in Britain are the Championship Shows where Challenge Certificates can be awarded. A dog must win three Challenge Certificates under different judges in order to gain the title of Champion.

The U.S.A. has, on average, ten times more shows than the U.K., but the numbers entered in individual classes are usually far smaller. As well as the scheduled A.K.C. dog shows, matches are also held, and these are usually for puppies of all-breeds. In order to compete in the U.S.A. your dog must be registered with the American Kennel Club, and it must be six months old before it is eligible to compete in Championship (or point) shows. To become a Champion a dog has to win a total of fifteen points, and at least two of the wins must be 'majors', with the dog winning three to five points, and these must be awarded under two different judges. The points are worked out on a State basis, and this is calculated according to the number of entries at the previous year's show. Therefore, the more dogs that are entered at a show, the more points that will be available for the following year's show. This obviously favours States and districts that have a stronger Papillon following, as more points are available in these regions. When a dog becomes a Champion it can only compete in special classes for new Champions, which leaves the way clear for other Champions to come through. Classes at shows are judged to find the Winner's Dog and the Winner's Bitch, and then points are awarded to the Champions in the special class. The winning dogs can then challenge for Best of Breed, and the dog that wins this can go forward to be judged in the Toy Group. Here, the judge places the final four in line, and the first prize winner goes forward to meet the other Group winners, competing for Best in Show. On the whole, American dog showing is a far more professionally orientated sport than it is in the U.K. Professional handlers are used extensively, although there are still many owners who handle their own Papillons. Professional handlers are very slick in the show ring, although it is always the handler that knows and understands the dog – whether he owns it or not – that is the most successful. Professionals are often enlisted because of the vast distances that have to be travelled in the U.S.A. in order to campaign a dog. Some exhibitors favour motor homes, while others prefer to fly to the different locations. The principal shows are organised so that you can arrive at a venue at the start of a weekend, and in the course of a couple days there will be two or three shows in close proximity.

If you are exhibiting your Papillon, daily care is as important as the last minute preparations

*The grooming box should be packed the day before a show.*
*Pearce.*

before the show. The dog must be in top condition – both inside and out – in order to succeed in the show ring. Correct diet is essential for the dog's physical appearance and well being. It should be exercised regularly to keep it fit, and you should make sure that this includes a little road work, i.e. walking on a hard surface, as this helps to keep the dog toned up and firm in muscle, and it keeps the pasterns strong. Finally, the dog should be groomed daily to keep its coat in top-class condition, and its ears, mouth and feet should be checked regularly so that you spot any minor problems before they develop. You must also ensure that its training sessions have been fun, and then you will have a happy and alert dog to take into the ring to show off its breed type and virtues.

The day before the show, your Papillon will need to be bathed, and you will need to check its nails and see if the hair between the pads needs trimming. Pack a bag ready with all the equipment you will need such as grooming equipment, leads, titbits, water for the dog to drink, a

*Exhibitors should be dressed smartly, but you have to be prepared for all weathers!*
*Dave Freeman.*

*Judge Pamela Cross Stern making her final assessment.*

kitchen roll, a ring clip to put your ring card in, plus whatever food and drink you will need for yourself! It is easier for men to decide what to wear in the ring, as long as they look smart. But women should stop and think of the problems caused by a billowing skirt or a dress that is going to flap in your dog's face and probably hide most of its body from the judge. Wear smart shoes, but avoid high heels – not only would these be dangerous if you stepped on your dog, but you will find it difficult to move on uneven or muddy ground if the show is outside.

It is very important to keep calm and collected when you are at a show. Listen to the loudspeaker announcements so you do not miss your class, and try not to get too nervous, as this will transfer to your dog. Make sure your dog has been to the exercise area to relieve itself before it goes into the ring, and allow the dog a few minutes to have a look around before you are due in the ring. When your class is called, go into the ring and collect your number from the steward and attach the card where it will be readily visible. Then, stand in a line with the other exhibitors and pose your dog, as you never know when the judge is looking at your dog. The

*Daneview Dainty Yulara, owned by Mrs Anna Mcknight, winning her third CC, to become a Champion, and Best of Breed winner, Swedish Ch. Smaragdens Kicking Up Ruby Wings At Ringlands, with judge David Roe.*

usual procedure is for the judge to walk down the line of exhibits to have a look at them, and then to ask everyone to walk round in a circle. This is a good idea as it helps the dogs to settle down. The judge will then examine each dog individually on the table. When the exhibit in front of you has been moved off the table ready to move, put your dog on the table so that it is ready as soon as the judge has finished looking at the other dog. Some judges will ask the dog's age, so have this information ready. When the judge has examined your dog on the table, you will normally be asked to move your dog in a triangle and then up and down in a straight line, and finally to stand your dog correctly on the floor while the judge has a good look at it. Judges will often try and get the Papillon to 'use its ears' – moving them forward so they are fully erect. When the judge has finished looking at your dog, return to your place and make a fuss of your dog, but always keep an eye on the judge. When the judge is going over the last dog, make sure your dog is ready 'to show', so you are both prepared when the judge walks down the line and is deciding on the placings. If you are lucky enough to get pulled out and win a card, well done! If not, there is always another show. However, it is important to remember that you are in the ring for somewhere between five minutes and fifteen minutes, and for two of those minutes the judge is looking at your dog, and that you have spent a considerable time in preparing for the show, plus the time spent travelling to the show – so do put all your concentration into showing your dog, rather than chatting to your neighbour. If you worked out how much those two minutes cost in terms of entry fees, catalogues, petrol, coffee, sandwiches, shampoo etc., you would probably be horrified!

American shows are run on similar lines to a U.K. Championship Show. There is an area for grooming and preparing your exhibit, and just before your class you have to report to the ring steward and collect your ring number, which is worn on your arm. In the ring there is a judge and another steward, who hands out the ribbons to the winners. The judge examines the dog on the table, and then the exhibitor is asked to move the dog so that the judge can assess movement and conformation. When all the exhibits have been individually assessed, the judge must decide on the placings. Handlers will stand in line, and they are allowed to 'top and tail' their dogs – the exhibitor is usually in a kneeling position and holds the dog's head up by a short, taut lead, while the other hand holds or supports the dog's tail over its back. This form of handling is frowned upon in the U.K., where it is the custom to attempt a more natural pose. Natural handling is also used by exhibitors around the world, who share the British view.

A lot of people cannot understand why it is that a dog can win a first prize at one show, and then fail to win a first prize at the next show. The answers to this simple question are manifold, and it is important that exhibitors are aware of all aspects of competing in the show ring. Firstly, beauty is in the eye of the beholder, or in our case the judge, and it is a matter of how one individual interprets the Breed Standard. The result will depend on what dogs are in the class, and on your own dog. It could be that your dog has dropped some coat, or maybe it is feeling off-colour; it could be too hot, too cold, too windy, or too noisy. The reasons for failing to win are endless, but one thing is certain, everything must be going right for you on the day you win. The challenge for regular showgoers is to have your dog looking and feeling at its best, and then trying to get the very best out of your dog. Every dog has its faults, and it is up to the judge to try and assess your dog's good points and to weigh up its faults against the other competitors. However, if you get the showing bug, life will never be quite the same again. We love every minute of it, but it is important to bear in mind that it is very time-consuming, and can be very tiring for both humans and dogs – but it really is a great hobby!

# Chapter Eight

# THE PHALENE

The Phalene is the dainty drop-eared variety, and the Breed Standard requirements are exactly the same as for the Papillon other than stating that the ears must be completely dropped. The Phalene is a descendant of the Continental Toy Spaniel, and it is more Spaniel-like in expression than the Papillon. Some Phalenes are inclined to be heavier in type, both in head and in bone. However, there are some exquisite specimens which exemplify all that is best in the breed. Papillons are numerically far stronger than Phalenes, and the majority of litters are confined to erect-eared Papillons. However, it can sometimes be difficult to tell whether you have a Phalene in a litter. The two varieties look totally different when they are adults, but most puppies are born with their ears folded down. The situation is further complicated because some Papillons' ears go up very quickly, and others take much longer, leading you to think that you have a Phalene. The way to tell whether you have a true Phalene is to test the ear-leathers. In the case of a Phalene, they do not stand up at all, but must remain lying close to head. When the dog tilts its head back, there should be no sign that the ears could ever be erect; they should remain completely Spaniel-like. Many people make the mistake that they think that they have a Phalene when, in fact, they have a soft-eared Papillon. This occurs when the ears should go up, but for one reason or another, they fail to become erect. You can tell whether you have a Phalene or a soft-eared Papillon when the dog tilts its head back. If it is a soft-eared Papillon its ears will go into a nearly upright position, like those of an erect-eared Papillon.

When the Phalene was first introduced to Britain in the twenties it was roughly equal in

*Am. Ch Loteki Bounty Hunter.*                    *Darla Galam.*

*Skymmingen's Pirutte and Skymmingen's Liline, Champions in France, exported from the Skymmingen kennel in Sweden.*

*Mex. Am. Ch.
Firebird's Karb-
N-Kopi.*

*Ch. Firebird 's
Cherokee 11.*

numbers to the Papillon. Ch. Peterkins, a solid-headed dog, and Ch. Rudolph du Veurne both won their titles, but then the number of Phalenes rapidly dropped and it was the erect-eared Papillon that became more popular. It is now many years since a Phalene gained its title in Britain. However, both varieties were used in breeding programmes in order to enhance the breed, and so Papillons and Phalenes continued to be produced in the same litter. In fact, it is perfectly possible for two erect-eared Papillons to produce a Phalene – and this does not mean a soft-eared Papillon, but a true Phalene. However, as the Papillon has grown in popularity it is becomingly increasingly difficult to brced Phalenes, as the erect-eared variety dominates present-day bloodlines. The result of this is that Phalene enthusiasts have to search through pedigrees in order to find evidence of Phalenes in the line, and then the strength of the Papillon is so dominant that two Phalenes mated together may well produce only erect-eared puppies. In order to stengthen the Phalene line, Mrs M. Pratt imported a couple of drop-eared dogs; the red and white Harilovon Kronblom and Harilovon Jonna. Mrs Kay Stewart imported the black and white Pierosas Albertina at Tussalud.

Phalenes are few and far between in the U.K. The Papillon Club has Phalene classes at its show, and the Northern and Eastern Club put on classes at one of their open shows. Occasionally, a Phalene will enter at an Open or Championship show along with the Papillons, but numbers are still very low. However, breed history was made when, at Crufts 2000, Sunshoo Imamovie Premiere won the bitch CC and Best of Breed. This was the first time a Phalene bitch had won the CC and the first time since the mid-twenties that a Phalene had won a CC. Her other two CCs followed in the same year at the City of Birmingham Championship Show, and her third CC, giving her title, at the Belfast Championship Show, so breed history was made twice in the same year. Maxine Moth, as she was known, actually had a litter before she commenced her show career.

Phalenes are more numerous on the Continent, where they are shown very successfully, with a number achieving their Championship titles. Sweden is undoubtedly the most progressive country; since 1967, it has had a separate classification for the Phalene, and many Phalene Champions have been made up since then. The first male Champion was Nord. Ch. Tunermarkens Clown Beppo, and the first female Champion was Lady. The first Phalene to become an international Champion was Svane Hills Lory. The Phalene has its own separate breed club, which was formed in 1976. However, problems can arise if you register a puppy as a Phalene and then the ears go up. In order to change the registration to a Papillon, the dog has to be examined by three judges of the breed to verify that it is now a Papillon. Likewise, if you register a Papillon and later it turns out to be a Phalene, the same process has to be gone through.

In the U.S.A., Papillons and Phalenes are both registered as 'Papillons'. However, Phalene classes are held at the Specialty Shows, and a few Phalenes have become Champions. The Phalene is small in number, but there is more enthusiasm for this variety, and, as a result, its future looks more promising than it does in Britain. Mrs Lou Ann King has done a lot for the Phalene, and she recently campaigned the red sable and white Phalene Ch. Loteki The Bounty Hunter to his title. In Canada, Clarice Babbidge campaigned the first Phalene Champion for sixteen years with American and Canadian Ch. Jaclairs Curb Stone Cutie.

# Chapter Nine

# PAPILLON COLLECTABLES

We have always been interested in Papillons of yesteryear and in the general history of the breed, and so tracking down Papillons in paintings, stamps and other artefacts is a most rewarding hobby. The range of Papillon collectables is quite varied – from cigar wrappers to Lladro porcelain. It seems that there is something about the delightful butterfly dog that has attracted artists throughout the ages. Dog shows are a good place to start hunting for collectables, as there are many stalls that specialise in Framed Philatelics, postcards, cigarette cards and prints. Obviously, all collectors want to try and find something that dates back in time, but some of the models, pottery and paintings that are being produced today are high in quality, and after all, modern-day collectables are tomorrow's antiques and we have some very talented people about. Rosa Wardle is well known for her beautiful embroidery, and each one of the Papillons that she embroiders is very easy to identify. Malcolm Green's work is known to many through newsletters and cards, and he clearly has a good sense of humour, judging by some of his cartoons. The artist Deirdre Ashdown has the gift of capturing the individual characteristics of every dog that she draws, and her work is known worldwide. Sue Jones is also making a name with her miniatures, and we are lucky enough to own two of these. Sue has also done some glass engraving, which is very effective indeed.

Papillon collectables often reveal new aspects of the history of the breed, and recently we saw

*Two tri-coloured Papillons, embroidered by Rosa Wardle.*

*Dremas Double Maxim of Sunshoo and Sunshoo Imadreamer, painted by Deirdre Ashdown.*

*A cartoon by
Malcolm Green.*

some fascinating material featured in an old brochure of the Dog Museum in Boston, Massachussets. The brochure itself is a collectable and features some very rare pictures. It also has a Breed Standard for the Epagneul Papillon Butterfly or Squirrel Spaniel. It states:

*"Two names for one breed: Butterfly in comparison to its ears, and squirrel in comparison to its tail.*

*General Appearance A Lively and active Ladies dog.*

*Ears Set On High at The head carried like the wing of the butterfly or hanging and always heavily feathered.*

*Tail Long. Carried like the squirrel well over the back and heavily feathered.*

*Colour Self-coloured red mahogany, ruby, chestnut red, dark yellow or white with these patches.*

*Height at shoulder from 8 to 10 inches, the smaller the better."*

   Unfortunately this brochure is not dated, but it is very well illustrated and features a number of photographs, and is written in a number of different languages.


CIGAR WRAPPERS

We have discovered four of these. Two of them are from Willem II's time, and these show a red and white Phalene and a very pretty red and white Papillon, who is very typical of the breed. Drido shows a small photograph of a black and white Pap from the Europa Show, again a very typical dog, and finally there is Washington, which is a study of a black and white Papillon.

*A selection of cigar wrappers.*

*A selection of cigarette and trade cards.*

## CIGARETTE CARDS

Papillons did not often feature on sets of cigarette cards, but John Player issued one in 1931 in a series called *Dogs* by Arthur Wardle, and it shows a red and white Papillon on a white background. Gallaher issued a set in 1938, and this features a study of a sable and white Papillon standing in a room. Godfrey Phillips had a series which they called *Our Dogs,* and this shows a Papillon puppy standing. This card was available in three sizes because the cigarettes came in packs of ten, twenty and fifty. John Sinclair Ltd issued *Champion Dogs* in 1938 and 1939, and this card was issued in two sizes. It shows Ch. Offley Beau Ideal, owned by Mrs Langton Dennis. Beau Ideal was born in 1935.

## JEWELLERY

We have never been lucky enough to find any antique jewellery featuring a Papillon. However, there are some very tasteful pieces being made now. There are full figures of Papillons in gold, which were made by an enterprising jeweller, who lives in a small village in Lincolnshire. Gingerberry Design specialise in making canine jewellery, and commissions to feature individual dogs are accepted. Studio Danielle is also producing some nice pieces, which excel in capturing the daintiness of the Papillon.

## MODELS

Compared with some of the popular breeds, there are few models of Papillons and they can be extremely hard to get hold of. However, there are a number that are more readily available. Northlight have produced a small model of a Papillon standing, which is very typical of the breed, and is available in three colours: red and white, black and white and tri. They also do a bronze resin model of this. Some time ago they brought out a very large model of a Papillon sitting, with a front paw held up. This was a limited edition and was quite stunning. Papillon enthusiasts worldwide have bought these models.

It is very difficult to get hold of models made by Bazil Matthews. They are small and very distinctive, and there is a certain amount of artistic licence with his models. We have two: one of a red and white Pap lying on a cushion, and a very small one of a Pap sitting on a cushion. Elizabeth Knowles, known to everyone in the British Papillon Club and to many people overseas, used to take commissions for Papillon models, and we are lucky enough to have two: one is of Stouravon Luanda At Sunshoo, a black and white, and the other is Fircrest Frivolity Of Sunshoo, a red and white who is now an American Champion. Peter Benson, son of Edith Benson and the late Ben Benson, has done some wonderful work over the years for the Papillon Club, including a lovely bronze resin model of a Papillon standing. There were just a limited number of these made for sale through the Papillon Club. The club had a special model commissioned for their Jubilee Year celebration, and this was of a Papillon lying down.

Most collectors go to dog shows or antique shops in search of Papillon items, but sometimes they can turn up in the most surprising places. We were on holiday one year in the Balearic Islands and we found a set of three Papillons, consisting of two adults and one puppy, and these

*Models by Bazil Matthews.*

*'Two sitting Papillons': the larger model is Neo Lladro, the smaller is Lladro.*

*'Girl holding Papillon': Neo Lladro.*

*Ceramic plastic Papillon made between 1930 and 1940 by Amery C. Simons, now in the Dog Museum in St Louis.*

'Papillon Family' made in Taiwan.

'Windblown', a
limited edition of 60,
by the American
sculptress Nancy
Miller Pinkie.

'The Butterfly Dog', a limited edition of 60, by Nancy Miller Pinkie.

were made in Taiwan! We also collect Lladro porcelain, which is made in Spain, and the Papillon is featured in a number of their models. One of the well-known pieces is a tall elegant lady, with a Papillon sitting at her feet. There is also a separate model of the dog, which is on a slightly larger scale. There are some stunning pieces, which can be bought for many hundreds of pounds, such as the Vintage Car full of passengers with a Papillon sitting on its mistress's lap, and a model of a very elegant lady leaning over a balustrade, with a Papillon looking up at her. There are a number of models made by Border Fine Arts, and some very beautiful and unusual models made by Zelli. Sylvia Smith has also quite an extensive collection of Papillons, from single Paps lying down to a group of five playing. One of the most beautiful models in my collection is by the American sculptress Nancy Miller Pinkie – she has captured the very spirit of the Papillon. Nancy, who works under the name L'Image, is helped by Susan Cassern. All their Papillon models are limited editions and the moulds are broken after the numbers have been made. Nancy says of her work: "Creating bone and muscle out of clay – creating a sculpture – is like creating a live dog."

MUGS

There are not many Papillon mugs on the market, but those that are available are of good quality. Peter Benson made some beautiful mugs with a Papillon head in relief; these are really exquisite. We have also seen a very nice mug made in America, which features a number of Papillons getting up to all sorts of antics. The Papillon Club of Great Britain and the Papillon Club of the Netherlands had their own mugs made, and there are likely to be a lot more clubs following their example. Dalsetter Design have made a pretty bone-china mug and are now going in for plates and teapots.

*Breed Club mugs: the Netherland Papillon Club (left) and the Papillon Club of Great Britain.*

*A print of a French engraving, which shows a Papillon under the stairs.*

POSTCARDS

These are quite scarce, and the majority come from France, with some from Italy, Belgium and Germany. In most cases they are reproductions of paintings rather than photographs. We have found one set of six cards, which shows a young boy and girl and a Papillon, some taken inside a house and some taken out in the snow. However, we have discovered that the Papillon was not a live dog, but a stuffed model. We have two beautiful postcards, which appear to be painted from life: one is of a Papillon 'Mirza', who was owned by van den Heer J. Mejis Maastricht, and the other is 'Byou', owned by Fraulein J. Chene of Paris.

PRINTS

*Hutchinsons Dog Encyclopedia* has a lovely head study of a Papillon which was done by Scott Langley and is dated 1934. There is another print which is available called *Guess Again* by the artist Sophie Anderson (1823-1898). This print appeared on the front of *Forbes Magazine* in the U.S.A., and it shows two little girls, one sitting down and one standing behind her, and covering her eyes up. There is a rather large black and white Papillon standing on its hindlegs

*Print of a Phalene,
by an unknown artist.*

*Stable scene, featuring a Papillon, by an unknown artist.*

*A selection of stamps featuring the Papillon.*

with its front legs on the chair, looking at the two girls. If you are lucky you may be able to get hold of a print or a postcard of Malcolm S. Tucker's *Dog with a Box*, dated 1893, which was presented to the Dog Museum in St. Louis by Mrs L. Lola. There are a number of old prints, which are unfortunately un-named and undated, including a lovely picture of a stable scene with a horse and a black and white Papillon. There is another print of a red sable Phalene which has the most lovely and typical expression. G. Vincent Anglade painted a head study of a shaded sable with the tip of its tongue sticking out, and this is apparently dated 1930. A Scraperboard print by R. Russell (1977) also depicts an excellent head study.

STAMPS

There is now quite a collection of stamps which feature Papillons, and some are from the most unexpected countries. Mongolia has stamps depicting a Papillon head study and two Paps performing in a circus. Kampuchea and Nicaragua have used Papillons on their stamps. One of my favourites is from Dhufar, and shows a Papillon head study.

TRADE CARDS

Edward Sharp & Son issued a set of *Prize Dogs,* which included Mounchy, a Papillon. However, looking at the card itself, the dog appears to be a Phalene. The Molassine Co. (pet food) had a series of cards called *Puppies;* this shows a puppy with an adult's head in one corner. Weetabix issued a set of 3D cards to be looked at through a viewer, and these featured two Papillons, a tri-colour and a black-and-white; this was from a series called *Working Dogs*, and it appears that the two Papillons are standing in front of small carriage. One of the loveliest cards was issued by the Observer Picture Cards, which were printed in conjunction with the Observer Books. These were not give-away cards, like most of the trade cards; they had to be purchased. The Papillon that is featured is a delightful red and white, and the artist's signature appears to be Butler. Very rare among trade cards are those issued by Nestles Chocolate in the twenties. The pictures were printed on gummed paper, and a Papillon is pictured with a Pug.

The range of collectables that you can buy featuring Papillons is growing all the time, and this seems to be a trend that is likely to continue. Among the more unusual items in our collection are a set of wind chimes, which are made up from five individually made Papillons, and tapestry, wooden goblets, featuring a Papillon's head. Obviously, the items that you choose to buy depends on personal taste, but if you have the collecting bug, you will be happy to buy anything – as long as it features a Papillon!

# Chapter Ten

# PAPILLONS IN NORTH AMERICA

Papillons are members of the Toy Group, and although they are not numerically the strongest breed in the Group, they have an enthusiastic following. The breed was officially recognised by the American Kennel Club in 1915, and in 1935 the first Papillon Club of America was formed. In 1954, at the first post-war show, there was an entry of forty-three dogs, and Best of Breed went to Am. Ch. Ywain Of Dulceda, owned by Mrs Kemmerer. Today there are a handful of breed clubs located around the country, and they are all affiliated to the parent club – the Papillon Club of America. The Secretary of this club keeps a list of breeders for prospective owners, and this is the best way to track down a puppy if you are a newcomer to the breed.

The size of the country has led to considerable variation in the size and type within the breed. This is largely because Papillon breeders are so widespread that it is difficult to form a common gene pool – even though everyone is governed by the Breed Standard. If you want to become a judge you have to meet certain qualifications and pass various tests administered by the American Kennel Club. Obviously an aspiring judge can learn a lot from this process. It is equally important to have an eye for a dog, and that is something that it is impossible to teach. There are not a great number of All Round Judges in the States, and the emphasis is on judging specific breeds, rather than building up a repertoire of breeds that you are qualified to judge.

Obedience competition is an extremely popular occupation in all breeds, and it is surprising how successful the Papillon has been in this field. The first grade to achieve is Companion Dog (CD), working up to Utility Dog (UD). There are quite a number of exhibitors who show Papillons, and also compete in Obedience trials, and a number have gained the CD qualification. In order to gain the title Obedience Champion a dog must gain one hundred points, and then it can carry the letters OTCH in front of its registered name. This entails a lot of hard work and dedication, but a number of Papillons have achieved this distinction. The Mariposa kennels, belonging to Virginia Newton, have housed many show Champions, who have also excelled in Obedience. They include: Ch. Coquet Of Mariposa CD, Ch. Triumph Of Mariposa CDX, Ch. Venice Of Mariposa CD, Ch. Sparks CD, Ch. Nimber, Ch. Gowdy & Etienne Of Mariposa CD. In fact, Viginia's first Papillon, Lancelot Of Dulceda, became the first Champion in the breed with an Obedience title, the second CD, and the first CDX. In 1953 Admiral Of Mariposa became the first Papillon to gain the UD title, with six perfect scores. Dr John Evans, of Portland, Oregon, trained a total of nineteen Papillons who won Obedience titles, including Ch. Elizares Sante UD and Vivette des Sapins UDT. Vivette became the breed's first UDT in 1966, and remained the only tracking title holder for ten years. Dr Evans also bred the second Papillon to win the UD title, Bateleur des Sapins. The Carousel Papillons made a name for themselves at this time with the trio of Champion UD Papillons: Ch. Neat N Tidy Of Carousel, Ch. Witch Doctor Of Carousel and Ch. Zorro Of Carousel.

In the sixties the numbers competing in Obedience increased by nearly 400 per cent, as more and more Papillon owners wanted to test their dog's intelligence. The outstanding dogs were Stouravon Martyne's Autumnal Gloric UD, owned by Arlene Czech, and Quincy Of Carousel UD, owned by Karen Hubbs from Northern California. This Papillon was also certified in tracking, but illness prevented him from winning the breed's second TD title. Bruce and Sally Genthner's Pierre de la Rouge became the first Papillon to win a UD title in the US and Canada, also winning the Papillon Club of America's Obedience Award for two successive years. David and Donna Elizares, of Oregon, have been active in Obedience competition for many years, and their outstanding Papillons include: Ch. Spicer's Royale Rascal UD, Ch. Werther des Sapins UD, Ch. Elizares Mamme UD, and Elizares Play Boy UD, who won the Papillon Club Of America's Obedience Award for two successive years. Beth Donnelly and her daughter Sharon, now Mrs Wenzel, enjoyed almost instant success when they switched from training Toy Poodles in Obedience to training Papillons. Kora Of Mariposa, better known as 'Mouse', was a UD and a Champion by the time she was seventeen months of age, and then gained both titles in Mexico. Her daughter, Parisienne Of Papilo, earned the UD title in the US and Mexico and went on to produce three UD daughters in one litter. They were based in Southern California, and when Kay McDonald's show Papillons started to excel in Obedience, it created a stronghold of dual-purpose bloodlines. The outstanding Papillons of this era were: Ch. Florentine's Camille UD, Ch. Pamela Of Bannahyde UD, Ch. Elran's Mimi de Charweb UD, and Ch. Tawame's Little Dream. Bob Adams campaigned three Papillons to the new Obedience Trial Champion: Chasseur des Anges, the first member of the Toy Group to earn the title, Adams Racer of Bannahyde and Pacer of Waynesong.

The Elizares took a break from exhibiting, but their place was taken by Florence Godfrey, whose Papillons enjoyed great success in the Obedience ring. Fine Bird Of Mariposa won a UD

*Eng., Am. and Can. Ch. Daneview Gordon Highlander.    Rich Bergman.*

*Ch. Maximillian Betty Boops.*

title, followed by Bird's son, Titian's Thunder Bird UD, followed by a string of dual-purpose winners. Also in the Northwest, Bonnie Nichols trained Ch. Finikin's Charley Horse to be the first Papillon to win a dual Championship title. When Donna Elizares returned to the ring she immediately made an impact with OT Ch. Elizares Whiz-Bang, who went on to win the Papillon Club Of America's Obedience Award for four consecutive years. On the east coast Sheila Kulak took Benjerbo's Franshe Topaz and Le Duc's Fraternite to their UD titles, and Shirley Schwartz had the dual-purpose Papillons, Ch. Starheirs G Wil-O-Wisp and Ch. Starheir's Amanda Blaze. There was a renewed interest in Tracking when Carolyn Wells added the TD title to Ch. Starheir's Gypsy CD, and then Tracy Halverson trained the first Papillon to become a Champion UDT with Ch. Kavar Athena's Nimbo UDT. This success was repeated by Isla Sternberg's bitches Ch. Arbeitsheim's Choice Chablis and Ch. Stouravon Burghbridge Princess Suki. Isla handled her dogs to their titles from a wheelchair. A daughter of Isla's Ch. Chablis UDT became the breed's first TDX title-holder. This was Ch. Kine-Ahora Chasse CD, shown by Beverley

*Mrs Pat Groff with Am. Ch. Daneview Julio and Am. Ch. Daneview Betty Boops.*
*Don Petrulis.*

Jones in Florida. Papillons make ideal therapy dogs and in some states this scheme has been taken a step further. If a dog is found to have a suitable temperament, it is neutered and then placed in homes to live in alongside the residents. This has proved to be of great value to the elderly who may have lost the companionship of a much-loved dog when they came into the home. The resident pet can be taken out for walks, fed, and groomed and it soon becomes an integral member of the home.

There are many famous Papillon show kennels in the United States. There are quite a number of dogs which have been sent out from the U.K., and some of these dogs are behind the Papillons that are currently finding success in the show ring. Papillons bred by Mrs D. C. Gauss of the Cadaga kennels go back to the sixties, and in 1966 and 1967 Ch. Cadaga Kerry was the winner at Westminster and at the Specialty show, and was also top winning Papillon in 1966. Ch. Stouravon Blue Tammy was imported from the late Mrs Doreen Harris, and proved to be a very dominant stud dog, who certainly left his mark on future generations of Papillons. Mary Spector, of the Viktoria prefix, imported English and American Ch. Melchester Bowman Of Lordsrake from the British kennels belonging to Pauline Abbott. American Ch. Melchester Jacob was sent out from Britain to the United States by the late Mrs Madaline Wheeler – Jacob was litter brother to Ellis Hulme's Ch. Melchester Laura Of Tongemoor – and George and Netta Henderson sent out the British-bred Ch. Ragatina Of Inverdon. American and Canadian Ch.

*Ch. Dancibee Rigadoon, winning the Toy Group, owned by Dr and Mrs Lola.*

Kenrennie Udell was the foundation stud dog of the Debonair Kennels owned by Sally and Harold Fell. Pat Groff of the Maximillan Papillons is no stranger to the dog world, having made up Champions in other breeds before concentrating on Papillons. She is also a professional groomer, which must be an asset to any show kennel. Pat has made up many American Champions, and has also imported stock from the U.K., including English Ch. Daneview Gordon Highlander, bred and exported by Anna McKnight. Pat is a regular visitor to Britain, where she is well-known in Papillon circles.

Mrs Pearl George, of the Kvar Papillons (fomerly known as Kavar), is one of the leading American breeders and exhibitors of Papillons, and well over fifty Kvar-bred Papillons have gained their American titles. A number of these dogs have also gained Obedience titles. Her best-known Papillons include: American, Canadian and Mexican Ch. Rosecroft Pirouette, who was bred by Miss J. Ploughright in Britain and was exported to the United States along with Ch. Quinetta Athena. (The offspring from this pair included Champions Kvar Baza Mamu, Athenas, Mark CD and Frost E Flame.) American and Canadian Champion Kvar Baby Bronco, co-owned with Mary Jo Loye, was a highly successful tri-colour, Ch. Kvar The Huntsman was a vibrant red and white, a Best in Show and Papillon Club of America Specialty winner, Best in Sweepstakes, Best of Breed, and Papillon Club of America Gold Butterfly winner; Champion Kvar Fluff N Stuff made Champion number sixteen, followed by Champions Kvar Gone A Hunting, a Best in Show winner and Gold Butterfly recipient; Touch Of Josandre CD, Kvar Classic Josandre, Kvar Classic Gold Kvar. Champion Caswell Paper Tiger was bred by Jenny

*Ch. Kvar Touch Of Velvet (Am. Can. Ch. Kenrennie Selwyn – Kvar Touch Of Class).*

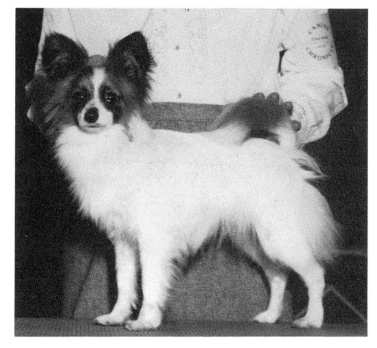

*Ch. Kvar L'Charm (Ch. Caswell Gay Cavalier – Ch. Kvar Candoo Chaparrel).*

*Ch. Loteki Autumn Magic CD: This bitch founded a dynasty of Champion Papillons.*                                    *Barb Zurawski.*

*Ch. Loteki Star Trek of
Kasway CD : a top
producer of high
quality Papillons.*

*Ch. Loteki Denzel
Fortuneteller: Toy
Group winner.*

*Tracy Halverson with Ch. Denzel Loteki Grand Illusion.*                    *Wayne Cott.*

Scovell in Britain and gained his title in the United States. The Loteki Papillons, owned by Lou Ann King, began with the arrival of Kvar Supernova in July 1978. Nova quickly became a Champion, and a multiple Group winner, and he was among the top ten Papillons for two consecutive years. The kennel's second Papillon, Papstedt My Sharonna arrived late in 1979, and became a dual Show Champion and gained her CD title when she was six years of age. Ch. Kvar Supernova sired thirteen Champions and Ch. Papstedt My Sharonna CD produced twelve Champions. Together, they produced five Champion offspring, including Ch. Loteki Autumn Magic CD, who proved to be a once in a lifetime breeder's dream. She set the record for most American Champions producing seventeen Champions to date, and these included four Group winners, three Group placers, and multiple Award of Merit winners, Sweepstake winners and point winners at Specialties. Judges agree that Magic passed on her 'look' to her progeny, and she was the winner of the 1986, 1987, 1988, 1990 and 1991 Greater Chicagoland Papillon Club Specialties. She lost this competition only once, and that was to her litter sister, Ch. Loteki Harvest Moon. Magic and her dam formed the first mother-daughter Dams of Distinction, a title awarded by the Papillon Club of America. Magic's full brother, Ch. Loteki Star Trek Of Kasway CD, is also a top producer, siring thirteen American Champions from his first thirteen offspring. One of the highspots for this kennel was when a daughter of Magic, Ch. Loteki Denzel Fortuneteller won the Toy Group twice, at just ten months of age. She is proving to be a top producer in her own right, with three Champion offspring to date, plus Group placers and Specialty winners. The Loteki kennel follows a heritage of line-breeding on the Canadian Jaclair Papillons and the American Kvar Papillons, with influence from several recent English lines.

*Can. Am. Ch.
Kenrennie Selywyn:
a big winner in the
show ring and a
highly successful sire.*

*Am. Can. Ch.
Denzel Loteki As
If By Magic.*

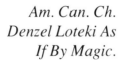

*Am. Can. Ch. Loteki Promise Me The Moon.*

The Denzel kennel, owned by Tracy Halverson and based in Columbine, Colorado, works in partnership with the Loteki kennels, and this has been to their mutual benefit. They co-own Ch. Loteki Autumn Magic, and regularly co-operate in breeding programmes. The Denzel Papillons started in 1983, and to date the kennel has produced over forty American show Champions. Tracy is also interested in Obedience training, and her first Papillon, Ch. Kvar Athena's Nimbo became the first in the breed to be a Show Champion, Utility Dog and Tracking Dog. The Denzel kennel has concentrated on producing Papillons of consistent quality in type and temperament, and English and Canadian Jaclar bloodlines have been influential. The foundation stud dog was Ch. Kvar Red Wings CDX, a Toy Group winner and sire of fourteeen American Champions. One of his offsping, Ch OTCH Denzel Loteki Top Secret TDX became the first Papillon to achieve the highest of all AKC titles available – Show Champion, Obedience Trial Champion and Tracking Dog Excellent.  One of Ch. Loteki Autumn Magic's most famous offspring was Ch. Loteki Denzel Svengali CD, multiple Toy Group winner and Highest Scoring Dog in Obedience Trial Awards; this is the first Papillon to be handled to these dual

*Can. Ch. Sunshoo Imalalique.*

achievements by the breeder-owner. Svengali was also Best of Winners and Best Puppy in Sweepstakes at the 1986 Greater Chicagoland Papillon Club Specialty, and is also the sire of Champions, including a Ch. UD. The Denzel kennels produced the top U.S. Papillon show bitch for 1990 and 1991, Ch. Denzel Loteki Grand Illusion, a Magic daughter by Ch. Dourhu Dandini, a British import. Bred, owned and handled by Miss Halverson, this dog is a multiple Toy Group winner, and was awarded Best of Opposite Sex at the 1991 Papillon Club of America and Greater Chicagoland Papillon Club Specialties.

## CANADA

British-bred Papillons have been influential in establishing the breed in Canada, and now a number of kennels are producing high-quality stock from their own bloodlines. Mrs Barbara Kenworthy, of the Kenrennie Papillons, imported Canadian Ch. Stouravon Bonny Legend from Mrs Doreen Harris in Britain, and she imported the British-bred Ch. Inverdon Lucinda from George and Netta Henderson. Lucinda went on to produce Ch. Kenrennie Joy and Ch. Kenrennie Jaquetta. Other Champions include Canadian and American Champion Kenrennie Giuseppe and Canadian and American Champion Gaston, American and Canadian Champion Fircrest Filomena, exported by the late Miss P. Frampton, and British Canadian and American Ch. Inverdon Sebert, also exported by the Hendersons. Sadly American and Canadian Ch. Kenrennie Chauncey died at the age of eighteen months, which must have been a great blow.

Ch. Tarantella Of Annacott was a top winning Papillon in Canada for Moira Ure. Michael and Dinah Hill, of the Akarana Papillons, also imported some stock from Britain, and these included Ch. Thingden Topaz and Tortoiseshell, exported by Mr and Mrs Benson, and Ch. Quinetta Panito and Ch. Quinetta Concerto, who were exported by the late Mrs Joan Brown. Their other Champions include Akarana Panache, Pandemonium and Caprice. The Jaclair kennels, owned by Clarice Babbidge, has an impressive list of Champions. The kennel's foundation bitch was Costabrava Colette, bred by Mr R. D. Simpson and imported into Canada in 1965. She is the dam of Canadian and American Champions Letson, Jolie Jaqueline, Miss Expo, Deon, Marcus, American Champions Melody and Claudia, and Canadian, American and Bermudan Champion Jaclairs Karwartha Jason. Mrs Babbidge also had the first Phalene Champion for sixteen years with American and Canadian Ch. Jaclairs Curb Stone Cutie. The Hendersons exported Canadian and American Ch. Inverdon Michaela to Mrs Babbidge, just to add a few more Champions in the shape of Jaclairs Ziggy, Kimberlite, Howdy Doody CD and Jaunty Of Jaclair CD.

*Ch. Stouravon Elegant Mink (left): Crufts Best of Breed 1965, with Ch. Stouravon Green Jackets Mariner and Stouravon Sweet Memory, owned by Mrs D. C. Harris.*

# Chapter Eleven

# PAPILLONS IN THE BRITISH ISLES

There are a number of British Papillon breeders that have had an influence on the breed, both in the past and at the present time. Papillons are currently enjoying a wave of popularity, and although numerically they cannot be compared with the leading members of the Toy Group – the Cavalier King Charles Spaniel and the Yorkshire Terrier – there is a growing interest in the butterfly dog: the average entry at a Championship Show is around one hundred, and this covers quite a range in type.

Mrs. Norma Staff and her daughter Pat Munn, of the Ringland prefix, have bred, shown, imported and exported Papillons over many years. They have both judged the breed at Crufts, as well as overseas, and their knowledge of the breed is extensive. In 1953 Norma made the first post-war importation from Brussels, and this was Ringlands Adrien Du Petite Paon. Sadly he was killed not long after leaving quarantine, but luckily he had sired a couple of litters. In the sixties Norma exported Ch. Ringlands Pied Piper to the USA, and he went on to become the breed's one and only triple international Champion, gaining his title in Britain, the USA and Canada. At around the same time Norma purchased another import, this time from California. This was Danaidae Beauasacq d'Royal, known as Jamie Beau. In the seventies Norma exported the solid-headed Ch. Ringlands Patternmaker to Australia, and the bitch gained her title over

*World Champion (British, Swedish and American) Smargdens Kicking Up Ruby Wings At Ringlands, imported by Mrs Norma Staff from Sweden.*

*Thomas Fall*

*Ringlands Elegant Emilia At Flutterbye, a daughter of Ch. Smargdens Kicking Up Ruby Wings At Ringlands.*

*Pearce.*

there. In the eighties Norma imported Elegant Boy Of Silver Riding At Ringland from Japan. This dog was bred by Mr Y. Baba, but he was sired by one of Norma's own dogs, Japanese Ch. Ringlands Spring To Mind out of the Swedish-bred bitch Pierosa Benedictine. Although Elegant Boy was only shown in Britain a couple of times, he has made his mark as a sire. He is a very distinctive stud dog, and there are now a number of quality Papillons descended from him, and from one of his sons, Ch. Ringlands Hal. In the late eighties Norma imported a dog from the Swedish kennels of Bibi Lundberg. Swedish Ch. Smaragdens Kicking Up Ruby Wings At Ringlands, known as Emil, was campaigned in Britain, and gained his title, becoming the first Swedish and British Champion. Before he came over to England he was busy as a sire in Sweden, and he has Champion offspring over there (Papillons and Phalenes), as well as an Obedience Champion, so he has passed on brains as well as beauty. He was much in demand for stud duties in Britain and sired some successful litters before being exported to the USA. He has now gained his American Champion, becoming the first Swedish, British and American Champion.

It is a very expensive business to import dogs into Britain, as not only is there the expense of purchasing the dog and transporting it, there is also the added expense of six months in quarantine. This is a difficult period for the dog, and the owner has to be prepared to visit the quarantine kennels regularly, so that the dog does not become withdrawn and miserable. Obviously, a great deal of thought has to go into a breeding programme, building up successful bloodlines and periodically importing fresh stock, so it is no wonder that the Ringlands affix is known worldwide. Norma and Pat have had many beautiful dogs in their kennels, and these include International Ch. Ringlands Fircrest Figaro (Figaro features in the pedigree of Norma's last two imports, Elegant Boy and Ruby Wings), Ch. Ringlands Polly Flinders, British, Australian & N.Z. Ch. Ringlands Red Link, British, Australian & N.Z. Ch.Scarlet Ribbons, Ch. Ringlands Fairy Doll, Ch. Ringlands Red Ribbons, and Ch. Ringlands Hal, plus many Papillons that have been exported to different parts of the world, and have gained their titles in their own countries. Norma's current favourite is Ch. Ringlands Stella Star.

Ellis Hume and his Tongemoor Papillons have certainly made their mark over the years. One of his most famous dogs was Ch. Pierre Of Oakridges. This was the top winning toy dog in 1974, and was Best in Show at the Welsh Kennel Club Show in 1974, which was a first for Papillons, making breed history. Pierre was also a notable sire and his offspring include: Ch. Prestar Watchimgo Of Tongemoor, Ch. Tongemoor Tiger Lily, Miss V. Hourihane's Ch. Amscor Pirouette, Ch. Astoria Snowbird Of Tongemoor (top winning Papillon of 1978 and bred by Mrs M. Jukes), Ch. Melchester Tarquin Of Tongemoor, Ch. Melchester Laura Of Tongemoor (both bred by the late Madaline Wheeler, but owned and shown by Ellis), Ch. Tongemoor Robin Hood and Ch. Tongemoor Pierrette. Ch. Tongemoor Miss Peppermint, a daughter of Ch. Tarquin, had the honour of being top winning Papillon in 1981 and 1982, and she won the Toy Group at Crufts in 1982. She was then the top winning bitch of all time, a record which she held for some years. Ellis is a much respected judge of the breed, and is also in great demand as an all-round judge, as he awards CCs in the Toy, Working and Utility groups.

Pauline Abbott and the Lordsrake Papillons have also had great success. Pauline says that the dog that really put her kennel on the Papillon map was Ch. Stouravon Rafiki Simba Of Lordsrake, bred by the late Doreen Harris (Stouravon), and campaigned to his title by Pauline.

*Int. Ch. (Britain and Japan) Lordsrake Fireball, bred by Pauline Abbott.*

Some of Pauline's other Champions include: Ch. Melchester Bowman Of Lordsrake (Charthamcoombe Ian ex Barleybright Lucinda), who was bred by the late Mrs M. Wheeler and later exported to the States, where he continued his show career; 'Lizzie', the beautiful black and white Ch. Lordsrake Eliz'beth Jubilee, the red and white Ch. Lordsrake Katyanna, and the sable and white Lordsrake Invoice. One of their promising youngsters, Lordsrake Joker, won two CCs, and sadly died at the age of three. Ch. Lordsrake Fireball, the glamorous red and white dog, was also campaigned to his title, winning a CC at Crufts under the late Ben Benson. He was then exported to Japan where he became an international Champion, having left some very promising progeny behind in the U.K. Pauline also has some Irish title-holders, and they include Lordsrake

*Waranz Port Au Prince Lordsrake: imported from Sweden and owned by Pauline Abbott.* *Gerald Foyle.*

Emblem and Nimrod. The Lordsrake kennels have made up over fifty-five Champions in Britain and abroad, and Pauline has judged in many countries, including Sweden, USA and Japan, as well as in Britain. She has also imported a dog from Sweden, Waranz Port Au Prince Lordsrake, who has been lightly shown in Britain and Ireland; but obviously introducing a fresh bloodline for future breeding is of the utmost importance.

Jenny Scovell of the Caswell prefix has a very successful kennel of Papillons, although the prefix is known worldwide for Pembroke Welsh Corgis, which Jenny's mother, Gladys Rainbow, bred under the Caswell affix. Jenny's first Champion was the sable and white Papillon, Ch. Hendikay Gaytime of Caswell. Other Champions include: Endora Lordsrake, bred by Mrs Pearl

*Lordsrake Opportunity: owned by Pauline Abbott.*

*Lordsrake Joker: owned by Pauline Abbott.*

*Swedish import Pierosas Rikard Lejonhjarta At Tussalud, owned by Mrs Kay Stewart.*

*Ch. Endora Lordsrake, owned and campaigned by Jenny Scovell.*

*Ch. Caswell Copper Tiger: Reserve Best in Show, Crufts 1991.*
*Sally Anne Thompson.*

*Ch. Tussalud Nickledeon, owned and bred by Mrs Kay Stewart.* *Marc Henrie*

Peacock; Ch. Dourhu Distinction Of Caswell, a black and white bred by Ruth Johnston; Melchester Mimi, a glamorous red and white bred by the late Mrs M. Wheeler; Ch. Silverstreak Lathonia, bred by Mrs Gwen Edmed; Ch. Geanzger Gay Camellia Of Caswell, bred by Rosa Wardle, and the legendary Ch. Gay Copelia, an exquisite red and white, who produced the Champions Classic Touch, Coppelita, Copernicus, Carminetta and Copper Tiger. The most outstanding of these are Ch. Coppelita, the breed record holder, and Copper Tiger, who won the Toy Group and Reserve Best in Show at Crufts in 1991 – quite a family!

The Blackpark kennel is a family affair, with Isobel Urquhart, her son Gordon and his wife Cathy all joint holders of the Blackpark affix. Some years ago Isobel exported Blackpark Dandy to West Germany, where he became World Champion. In more recent years top honours have gone to Ch. Blackpark Cameo, who won the Toy Group at Belfast Championship Show; the enchanting tri-colour Ch. Blackpark Emma; and Gaystead Velvet Night, who was bred by the late Joe Ironside and sired by Kay Stewart's imported Swedish dog.

*Ch. Daneview Yoho, sired by Ch. Ringlands Hal, owned by Anna McKnight.*

*Pearce.*

The Tussalud prefix of Mrs Kay Stewart has been added to the three dogs that she has imported from Sweden. The first was Pierosas Pain Blanc At Tussalud, who was imported from Siv Roos, and went on to win fourteen CCs. Later Pain Blanc's half-brother, Pierosas Rikard Lejonhjarta, came into the country. He was shown and won two CCs, but unfortunately he was attacked at a dog show by two large dogs; he needed surgery, and this put an end to his show career. However, he went on to become a successful sire, and his Champion offspring include Ch. Gaystead Velvet Night and Ch. Tussalud Nickelodeon, a Group winner at the Southern Counties Championship Show. The third import was Pierosas Albertina At Tussalud, the most exquisite and enchanting Phalene to be seen in Britain for a very long time. This bitch has also proved her worth in the nursery. Kay has also made up the tri-colour Ch. Amazing Luath of Inverdon.

Mrs Anna McKnight of the Daneview Papillons has produced a successful strain of Papillons which have won consistently over a period of years. It was not always easy for Anna to campaign her dogs as for many years she was based in Aberdeen, so she had to travel many hundreds of miles to attend each Championship show. However, Anna was tireless in her efforts, and the Daneviews have made up a string of Champions including the black and white Ch. Daneview Charleston, Ch. Daneview Dainty Flora Dora, Ch. Daneview Eulana and the American and British Ch. Daneview Gordon Highlander; the sable and white Ch. Dainty Gaiety Girl and Ch. Yulara, who won an incredible number of reserve Challenge Certificates before gaining her crown; and the red sable Ch. Daneview Yoho. The Daneview kennel is not large in numbers, but the quality of the dogs is always evident.

The Noveau prefix, belonging to Mike Foster and Mark Billinghurst, has also been very successsful. Their first Champion, Noveau Le Grand, was a son of Ch. Charthamcoombe Tristan, and their next Champion, Noveau Lord Of The Rings, another black and white, had the honour of going Best in Show at the Papillon Club Open Show at just ten months of age, and went on to win Best of Breed at Crufts in 1985. Ch. Caswell Principality was bred by Mrs Jenny Scovell and campaigned to his title by Mike and Mark. He won the Toy Group at East of England Show in 1988. They have also imported two dogs from Sweden in order to introduce fresh blood to their kennel.

Claire Ahern, of the Pipistrelle Papillons, is based in Howth, County Dublin, and she has made up many Irish Champions. These include: Ch. Pipistrelle Claire The Loon, Ch. Pipistrelle Cagney, and Ch. Stouravon More Honey, to name but a few. Fergus Cousins, also from Dublin, made up the Irish Ch. Ringlands Red Rice. From over the border, in Northern Ireland, Marian Sloan made up the black and white Irish Champion Sunshoo Imasophisticate.

## FAMOUS PAPILLONS

The first Papillon to win a round of hotly contested Dog World/Spiller Pup of the Year competition, was Mrs Pearl Peacock's red sable and white Alcala Chantilly Lace, who later went on to gain her crown. The next Papillon to win a round was Mr and Mrs Hutchings' Gerlil Colorado Kid, who also gained his title. The most recent Papillon to achieve this was Anna McKnight's Ch. Daneview Yulara, who won her qualifying heat at Leeds

There have been a select few Papillons who have won the Toy Group at Championship Shows, but only two have attained Best in Show at a general Championship Show and these were Mr Ellis Hulme's Ch. Pierre Of Oakridges and David and Carolyn Roe's Ch. Sunshoo Imacaptain Scarlet. Ch. Caswell Copper Tiger was a great ambassador for the breed when he was awarded Reserve Best in Show at Crufts. Sunshoo Imahigeldy Pigeldy was lightly shown in the U.K. before being exported to Canada. She arrived at the airport on a Tuesday; by the Sunday night she was a Canadian Champion, having won two Groups on the way! This is believed to be a breed record.

There have been some very dominant stud dogs that have left their mark on the breed. Mr Clem Wood-Davis's Ch. Charthamcoombe Tristan lists among his children: Ch. Fircrest Fanta of Sunshoo (owned by us); Ch. Daneview Charleston (Anna McKnight); Ch. Stouravon Fircrest Fernanda (the late Doreen Harris); Ch. Fircrest Fidelity Of Gerlil (Mark and Nancy Hutchings); and Ch. Fircrest Filemon (the late Miss P. Frampton, who was the breeder of the famous Fircrest dogs, and Mrs N. Hutchings). Norma Staff's Japanese import, Elegant Boy Of Silver Riding At

*Canadian Champion Sunshoo Imahigeldy-Pigeldy, who gained her title in record time.*

*Irish Champion Sunshoo Imasophisticate.*

Ringlands, has proved to be a very valuable stud dog, siring Anna McKnight's Ch. Daneview Dainty Yulara and Ch. Ringlands Hal, who also marks his type on most of his children. These include Ch. Daneview Yoho, who is a sable and white like his sire. Another litter bred by Norma also contained three sables and whites, and all three have gone on to win well. Known as the 'T' litter, they were: our own Ringlands Tansy At Sunshoo, Ringlands Tom Thumb At Flutterbye and Ringlands Thomas. Our own Ringlands Erik The Red At Sunshoo, before his untimely death, was a very dominant stud dog, siring the Best In Show Ch. Sunshoo Imacaptain Scarlet, his litter brother Ch. Sunshoo Imascarlet Encore, litter brothers Ch. Sunshoo Imaknight Crusader and Ch. Sunshoo Imaknight Errant, Ch. Daneview Dainty Roxanne At Sunshoo, Ch. Daneview George Gershwin and the litter sisters Sunshoo Imascarlet Erika at Gleniren and Sunshoo Imascarlet Ribbon, plus several overseas Champions.

Other outstanding stud dogs include Inverdon Aristocrat and Inverdon Ganymede, to name but two from this outstanding kennel; Grenmichels Bronco, the late Mrs Doreen Harris's Ch. Stouravon Greenjackets Mariner and Ch. Stouravon Elegant Mink; and the late Bob and Peggy Russell Roberts's Ch. Picaroon Urbino and Ch. Picaroon Soloman.

# Chapter Twelve

# PAPILLONS
# AROUND THE WORLD

The Papillon comes from Europe, but it has now become popular throughout the world. Obviously type varies considerably in different parts of the world, but generally speaking, quality remains good and breeders have remained true to all that is best in this highly appealing member of the Toy Group.

SWEDEN

Papillons have become very popular in Sweden, and the Swedes have achieved considerable success in their breeding programmes. So much so, that a number of Swedish Papillons have been imported to Britain, and have proved very beneficial to the breed. Siv Roos, of the Pierosas Papillons, has bred numerous Champions. The best-known include: Pierosas Speedy Gonzales, Pierosas No No Nanette, American and International Champion Pierosas Stardust, and the litter sisters Pierosas Ophiela and Pierosas Ocarina. Ingrid Ashberg, of the Swings prefix, is very keen on Obedience work and her red and white Papillon, Ceholms Decibella, became a Scandinavian show and Obedience Champion – quite an achievement.

Christina Hedman, of the Fly High Papillons, started her kennel with the foundation bitch,

*Int. and Nordic Ch. Fly High Concorde: the top winner in Sweden in 1984, and a highly successful sire.*

*Swedish Ch. Siljans Vip Diplomat, showing beautiful curtain fringes and a solid head.*

*Sw. Ch. Pepejas Charming Claudine: Best of Club Show in 1990.*

Nordic Champion Pierosas Chantelle. Other notable winners include: International and Nordic Champion Fly High Concorde; Ch. Pocitos Ida, a daughter of Concorde; and Ch. Beddis Adamant Alexander, who was line-bred to Concorde. The La Roccas Papillons, owned by Brigitta Westergren, include the American Champion La Roccas Jingle Bell and Swedish Champion La Roccas Flight 007. Marie Louise Stegfors, of the Pepjas Papillons, can boast the top winning dog, all breeds, with International Champion Pepjas New Generation. Her other Champions include: Charming, Claudine, and Nordic Champion Pepjas Happy Girl.

   The Emblems kennel, owned by Margareta Dahlgren and Karin Neren, has an impressive list of Champions, and these include the Scandinavian Champion Emblems Christopher, a solid-headed red sable and white dog; Ch. Emblems Christel; Ch, Emblems Ftatteeta, a red and white bitch by International & Scandinavian Champion Quinetta Dieter; Champion Emblems Christopher Robin, a red and white dog; and the top winning bitch of 1981, American and Scandinavian Champion Emblems Coral. Suzanne Tamm, of the Trolleliar prefix, campaigned International & Scandinavian Champion Ringlands Fircrest Figaro, International & Scandinavian Champion Trolleliar Mimi, and Ch. Suzette. Smaragdens Kicking Up Ruby Wings To Ringlands, a Swedish Champion and sire of winning progeny, went on to gain his British title before being exported to the USA Ch Smaragdens Poker Face and Ch. Lucinda Lace are just two of the lovely Champions owned by this kennel.

DENMARK

Lis Sharwany, of the Fleur De Lis Papillons, is one of the leading lights in this country. Her most successful dogs have been the tri-colour International, Luxembourg & Danish Champion Fleur De Lis Casanova, and an import, Ch. Ringlands Jolita. Peter and Kitty Sjong, of the Inkie kennel, bred the top winning female, International, Danish & Lux Ch. Inkies Sweet Irina. Their import, Ibstock A Misty For Me, became a Danish, Lux & Belgian Champion, and was top winning female in 1989. Per and Mette Olsen, of the Gallina Papillons, campaigned International Champion Gallina Nimbus to become a world winner in 1989. Their other Champions include: Gallina Ola, Nini, Garou, Gilda, and Gomet, who was top winning Papillon 1989 and 1990.

## SWITZERLAND

The Papillon is small in numbers in Switzerland, but some top quality dogs have been exhibited in the show ring. Mrs Yvonne Voeglin, of the Kerberos affix, has been the most successful and her best-known dogs include: Picaroon Florimund, World Champion Zapangu Salome (who won the title in 1977 and 1978), and International Champion Quinetta Swiss Miss, who together with International Champion Fircrest Frere produced a litter of three Champions: Kerberos Irma La Douce, Inspecteur and Illustre Pierrot.

## GERMANY

The El Mariposa kennels in Germany have both Papillons and Phalenes. In 1986 the Papillon, Caswell Picador, became World Champion. He was exported from Britain by Jenny Scovell, and joined International and German Champion Farfrae Loveday of Melchester, who was exported by the late Mrs Madaline Wheeler, and World Champion Blackpark Dandy, who was exported by Mrs Isobel Urquhart. The Phalene Blanca-Bonita El Mariposa was World Champion in 1986, and this dog also carries the title of International and German Champion.

## AUSTRALIA

The Papillon was introduced into Australia by Mrs A. Jacobson, a Pekingese breeder, in 1949. The first imports were from England and were the red and white male, Corleon Of Otter, a red and white bitch, Monamie Bernice, and a tri-colour bitch, Cresta Of Harleymeads. In 1951 a second male, Jasper Of Confryn, was imported from England. In 1954 Mrs Jacobson gave the bitch puppy Bunteen Mei Mei as a christening present to Mrs Thorn Clark's baby twins, and this was the foundation of the Tres Chik kennels – the first Papillon kennel in New South Wales. There were several other kennels founded on the Bunteen stock at around this time. In 1957 Mrs Boord, from Seymour, Victoria, imported two Papillons from England: the black and white male, Ringlands Bobby Bingo, and the red sable bitch, Ringlands Closburn Conte De Fee. She later imported the sable and white dog, Baluch Wee William, who was to have a major impact on the breed. The first Papillons exported from Australia went to New Zealand, and these were Tres Chik Pagliacci and Tres Chik La Pompadour, both red and white, exported by Mrs Thorn Clarke in 1957.

In the sixties three Papillon breeders emigrated to Australia: Mrs Burton (Summercourt), Mr and Mrs Wyper (Jacdorene) and Mrs Ivory (Erina), and they all imported British stock. Mrs Burton was also instrumental in getting the Papillon Club of New South Wales off the ground, and this was the only Papillon breed club for a number of years. The Summercourt stock also

*Ch Pohwaugh
Lorenze, aged 8
months*

helped to establish a number of new kennels. On the other side of the country, Mrs Peg Nussey, of the Nuvale prefix, imported Inez de Luvic in 1965 and the tri-colour dog, Ynyswyn Sweet Williamin, 1967. Mrs Campbell, of the Campbelldale Papillons, imported the tri-colour bitch Ynyswyn Oxney Fern. In the early seventies Mrs Te Laak imported English Champion Thingden Riseling, who was used extensively at stud, and it is thought that he was instrumental in improving coat and soundness in the breed.

Today, the Papillon goes from strength to strength in Australia. Obviously in such a vast continent, many Papillons never come into competition with one and another, and so type does vary a lot, as it would do in any such large country. The Jacaith kennels, owned by Glad Sheppard in Victoria, have boasted several Champions. In 1967 Ch. Cricaith Gay Cherie became the kennel's foundation bitch. She was bred by Mrs Street, and won Best of Breed at Melbourne Royal in 1974. She went on to produce many Australian Champions, including the great Ch. Jacaith Ladybird, who had an excellent show career, including winning Best in Show at New South Wales. She went on to produce two Best in Show winners, with her sons Ch. Jacaith Royal Red and Ch. Jacaith Rodger, as well as many other Champions. Cherie's grand daughter was Ch. Jacaith Marguerite, who was the first Papillon to win Best in Show in Australia. Other notable Papillons from this kennel include: the tri-colour Jacaith Jenny Wren, Ch. Jacaith Imacutie, who was made up at eight months of age, Imashow Girl, and the imported black and white Champion Sunshoo Imaprincess, who was Best in Show at the Victoria Papillon Club, and was the winner of two Brisbane Royals and the Challenge at the Melbourne Royal.

Dot Cooper of the Pohwaugh prefix has imported quite a bit of 'fresh blood' over the years, which has proved to be very successful, as Dot is very knowledgeable when it comes to

*Mrs Glad Sheppard's Ch. Jacaith Imacutie became a Champion at eight months of age.*

*Ch. Jacaith Imacutie (right), Panda the puppy, and Ch. Sunshoo Imaprincess.*

breeding. She has imported from the Ringlands kennels in the UK, including the stud dog Billy Bright Eyes Of Ringlands. Her home-bred Champions include Ch. Albagay Ricardo, who was out of Eng. & Aust. Ch. Thingden Riseling, Ch. Pohwaugh Silver Cort and Silver Belle Miyu Ima Jazzman. The Wenham kennel of Papillons, owned by Terry and Wendy Hamlyn, has also come to the fore and the black and white Champions Ch. Wenham Miss Muffett and Ch. Sunshoo Imadevil are among their outstanding winners. Peg Nussey, based in Western Australia, is well-known for her Nuvale Papillons. She only keeps a few dogs at the present time, but her winners have included: Ch. Nuvale Flashman, a red sable and white, Sunshoo Imacharmer, a tri-colour, Sunshoo Imadolly Bird, a black and white, and Blackpark Tanith.

Jean Rimmer in New South Wales owns the Jouetchien Papillons, and the first Papillon she owned, Kapel Pompidou, became a Champion. Her first success at home-breeding came with the litter brother and sister Jouetchien Mystique and Ch. Jouetchien Crispin; both were red and white. Ch. Jouetchien Blaque Fin and Ch. Jouetchien Glen Bracken were to follow. Jean also imported Ch. Harilovon Hippy Too from Mrs Pratt. Cath Wookey and Royce Walter, of the Alljo Papillons, come from Victoria, and they have made quite a name for themselves in the show ring. Their best dogs include Ch. Alljo Wild William, a tri-colour dog, and Ch. Alljo Frosty Menace. 'Menace' has enjoyed an excellent show career, and was Best in Show at the Victoria National Toy Dog Club Show, the Victoria Papillon Club Show and the Victoria Championship Show in 1989. David Bell of 'Papillons of Clochette' has had a string of Champions, and these include: Albagay Titania, Summercourt Gleam; the black and white dog, Clochette Crest; Clochette Cortot, also a black and white dog; the red sable dogs, Clochette Champagne and Claret; and the sable and white bitch, Clochette Chantilly.

## NEW ZEALAND

The Delzet Papillons, belonging to Syd and Leonie Hudson, are well known in this country. Their notable winners are: Ch. Delzet Martini, who gained his title at fourteen months of age, and the two Champion brothers, Delzet Amegos and Artemus. In fact, Artemus went on to gain his Australian title, campaigned by David Bell of the Clochette Papillons. The Farfalla Papillons imported Ringlands Micky Marmaliser, who gained his New Zealand title, and the British Champion Ringlands Scarlet Ribbon, who also gained her title in New Zealand.

## SOUTH AFRICA

The Bokara kennels, belonging to Geoff Jamieson and Mike Twoco, have specialised in Papillons, and their principal winners are Champions Lordsrake Howzatt Of Bokara, Lordsrake Half Penny Of Bokara, Mr T Of Bokara, Meziara Shady Lady Of Bokara and Bokara Chorus Girl, who had the honour of being Top Toy Dog in 1989. David Kytel, of the Littlewoods Papillons, has the Champion Gerlil Betina, and she is the dam of Ch. Littlewoods Robin Hood, Ch. Gerlil Miss Anna Marie and Ch. Charthamcoombe Titus, a son of the late Ch. Charthamcoombe Tristan.

# Chapter Thirteen

# BREEDING

Breeding should always be looked at in the long term: it can be very rewarding, but it can also be heartbreaking; it is amazingly time-consuming, but above all, there is always something new to learn. How often have you heard someone say: "Breeding a litter is fun"? We would answer that it can be, but not necessarily. Even more misleading is the person that says: "Every bitch should have a litter; it is good for her." This is complete rubbish, and if you are serious in your intention of breeding a litter of Papillons, you should be clear about why you want to do it. Some novices think that this is a way to recoup the money they paid for their bitch, or they think the sale of the puppies might provide a bit of pin-money. Neither is the case, and if you are going into breeding in the hope of making money, it is time to think again. However, if you are interested in improving the breed, and planning your own breeding programme – and you are prepared for a lot of hard work   then you are the right person to embark on this area of canine husbandry.

THE BROOD BITCH

The bitch that you plan to breed from should be typical of the breed, and free from any outstanding faults. She should be sound in body and mind, and she should be a reasonable size –

*Davandra They Call Me Mimi, was the foundation bitch for the Sunshoo Papillons. She is pictured with three Tibetan Terrier puppies, which she helped to rear after they were rejected by their mother. She even produced milk for them.*

*Ch. Caswell Gay Copelia: Best Brood Bitch in 1985, 1986, 1987, 1988 and 1989.*

neither a 'tiny' nor a 'giant'. The bitch's breeder is probably the best person to advise you in the choice of stud dog. The breeder will know the bitch's bloodlines intimately, and should have a fair idea of what to look for in a suitable mate. Obviously, you hope that your bitch is going to produce perfect puppies, but try not to get carried away! You must look at your bitch honestly, and if, for instance, she has not got particularly large or impressive ears, you will not solve the problem by looking for a stud dog with absolutely enormous ears, and forgetting about the rest of the dog. You will want a dog with good ears to try to improve this feature, but there are other important considerations. For example: Is the dog fine-boned, has he got a good topline, is his tail-set right? Look at the dog's pedigree, and try to find out what his parents look like, and his grandparents, if possible. However, it is important to always bear in mind that the best planned matings do not always produce exactly what you had hoped for. The resulting offspring may be bred in the purple, and the brood bitch and stud dog may both be excellent specimens of the breed, but nature can be unpredictable – sometimes for the good, but sometimes, unfortunately, not so good. This can be very frustrating, but it is what makes breeding such a challenge. You are always trying to think one step ahead: the moment a litter is born, you are looking for the puppy that could hold the key to your future breeding programme. Time and experience are invaluable in this business, and there is no substitute for either.

The bitch you are planning to mate should already have had one or two seasons, so you will know approximately when she will be due in season. Before this happens, you should worm her and ensure that she is in peak condition when she comes into season. A bitch can come into season any time between about six and eighteen months of age, although there is always the exception to the rule. The first signs of a bitch coming into season are usually small drops of blood coming from the vulva and the bitch is often preoccupied with keeping herself clean. As soon as she comes in season, contact the owner of the stud dog, and make an appointment in ten to eleven days time, when she should be ready for mating. The next stage in the season is when the vulva becomes puffy and swollen. The coloured discharge usually lasts for about eight to ten days, and then it gradually changes from being a blood-coloured discharge to a transparent pink colour. By about the tenth day the bitch's vulva will look quite large, and if you touch the area around the vulva she will swish her tail from one side of her back to the other, while standing firmly. Once she gets to this stage she is usually ready for mating. Most bitches are ready between the tenth and twelfth day, but some may be ready on the seventh day, and others may still produce a litter if they are mated on the twenty-first day. Some vets will take a swab, which will tell you exactly when the bitch is ready for mating. In this instance, the vet needs to be informed when the bitch has come into season in order to arrange the right time to do the swab-test. Some stud dog owners will insist that you have your bitch swabbed to protect their stud dog from getting an infection from a visiting bitch. If an infection is detected, the bitch can usually be treated with a course of antibiotics, and she should be clear by the time she is due for mating.

THE STUD DOG

The most important factors to consider when deciding whether a dog is suitable to stand at stud are identical to those when you are deciding whether to use a bitch for breeding. The dog must be sound in body and mind, he must be typical of the breed, and he should not have any outstanding faults. We always make a point of trying to see any puppies from our own stud dogs, to see if there are any faults that are coming through, or if the dog is particularly dominant in any particular breed point. This is the time to be completely honest with yourself: there is no point in advertising a dog at stud, if he is inferior in quality; after all, it could affect future generations of Papillons.

The stud dog owner also has a responsibility to the dog itself in terms of health and well-being, and you should never be frightened about putting the dog first when this issue is at stake. It may happen that you have agreed to a mating, and when the bitch arrives she appears unhealthy. In this instance you must refuse to allow your dog to be used, as infection can very easily be passed on and in a severe case it could make your stud dog sterile. The stud owner must also be prepared to assess the quality of the bitch before allowing a mating to proceed. If you let your stud dog mate a bitch of inferior quality or one that lacks true breed type, you are doing the breed a great disservice; and never forget, if the puppies do not come up to standard, it is invariably the stud dog that gets the blame.

If you own a stud dog, you must give careful thought to your breeding programme, rather than simply using your own stud dog when one of your bitches is ready for mating. Equally, do not choose a stud dog because it is kennelled at a convenient distance from your home. All serious breeders are hoping to produce puppies of quality, improving on breed points in existing bloodlines. However, it is important to remember that the puppies will inherit good and bad features from both parents, and so the time spent studying pedigrees will hopefully pay dividends. If you have a well-bred and typical looking bitch, most stud dog owners will be happy to talk to you about mating your bitch to their dog. Obviously there will be a stud fee to pay, but you will be bringing fresh blood into your own kennel, rather than constantly relying on

*Elegant Doy Of Silver Riding At Ringlands: imported from Japan and combining the best of British and Swedish bloodlines.*

the same lines, which tends to happen if you keep a stud dog specifically to use on your own bitches.

People are very often under the impression that a breeder will make a fortune by having a dog at stud: this is certainly not the case! Not only do you have the cost of keeping the dog and advertising it for stud duties, but all breeders will tell you that stud-work can be very time-consuming and difficult, especially if you have a maiden bitch who has decided that she does not want to be mated! Most stud dog owners will offer a repeat mating if the bitch does not come into whelp, but there is no obligation to do this. The stud fee is a payment for that service only, so make sure you are clear about the deal before proceeding.

## THE MATING

On the day of the mating, the brood bitch and owner will probably have to travel to the stud dog.

*Elegant Boy's son,
Ch. Ringlands Hal,
a very dominant sire
in his own right.*

*Ch. Ringlands Hal's daughter, Ringlands Tansy At Sunshoo.*          *Martin Leigh.*

When you arrive, give the bitch a chance to settle: give her a drink and let her out to relieve herself before she is introduced to the stud dog. Most stud dogs have a place where they like to mate their bitches, and each dog has his own way of approaching the job. Most like a bit of courtship – chasing the bitch around – before they get down to serious work. The dog will start to mount the bitch, and when he has actually penetrated, the bitch should be held steady. Once the dog has mated the bitch, the pair will normally tie for a period of time, which can be from two minutes to half an hour. The length of time they are tied makes no difference to the outcome, but most people believe that a good tie will improve the chances of a bitch becoming pregnant – although there are stud dogs that do not tie, but still get their bitches into whelp. There are no rules that cover matings, and some dogs will turn so they are standing back to back with the bitch, others prefer to stand side by side. Some bitches remain quite calm during this time, but others try to get away, or even try to bite the dog. It is important to ensure that both dog and bitch are held steady during the tie, as they may injure each other if they try to pull apart. When they have separated, put the bitch back into her travelling box to rest. Some stud dog owners offer a second service to the bitch, usually the day after the first mating. Stud fees are normally payable at the time of service.

## THE PREGNANCY

Hopefully, the bitch will be in whelp, and she should have her litter in approximately sixty-three days time. Some vets will do pregnancy testing between twenty-one and twenty-eight days, and this is done by palpating the abdomen. There is also a blood test to detect pregnancy, and some vets have an ultra scan which will also be able to give you a reasonable idea of the number of puppies the bitch is carrying. This can be very useful if you have a maiden bitch that is possibly carrying a very small litter – or even a single puppy – as it is almost impossible to find out if she is in whelp from any visible signs. Most bitches will show no physical changes for the first couple of weeks after being mated. When a bitch is about three weeks in whelp, she may go off her food or become very choosy about what she will eat. Occasionally, a bitch may be sick, or off-colour at this time. The nipples will usually become pink in colour, and they may start to protrude a little. She may have a clear but slightly sticky discharge from the vulva, but this can be difficult to see as most bitches will try to keep themselves very clean. The next sign is for the ribcage to become rounded and solid. The puppies are usually carried quite high up, and so the bitch will start to lose her waist-line and the ribcage and loin will 'thicken', so that she takes on a portly look.

If she is having a couple of puppies, you will be confident that she is in whelp after six weeks - it will be obvious just by looking at her. The hair along the edge of the ribcage appears to 'stand off' the body as she progresses into her pregnancy, the nipples become more developed and are usually a bright pink colour, and the bitch will often experience a change in temperament – she may become more loving and affectionate.

Food rations do not need to be increased until the bitch is five weeks into her pregnancy; the amount of food that is required depends on the individual bitch and the size of the litter she is carrying.

Fresh drinking water should be available at all times. Some bitches love their food and will make a pig of themselves, given half a chance. However, it is important to guard against the bitch putting on excess weight. She has the weight of the puppies and the placentas to contend with, and she should not be put under undue strain by getting too fat. The bitch needs to be as fit as possible when it comes to whelping, so let her have plenty of free exercise. She will know when she has had enough, and will be happy to rest when she is tired.

# Chapter Fourteen

# WHELPING AND REARING

Despite their small and dainty appearance, Papillons are healthy dogs, with no exaggerated breed points, and so whelping should be fairly straightforward. On average a bitch will produce a couple of puppies in a litter, although singletons are also fairly common. Obviously, there are exceptions, and we know of one Papillon who whelped a king-size litter of eight! When the bitch is about two weeks from her whelping date, it is a good idea to get everything ready for the big day. The first essential is to provide a comfortable whelping box so that the bitch can sleep in it and get used to it before she actually has her puppies. It must be large enough so that she can lie out at full stretch, and she must also be able to stand upright. The whelping box should be located in a warm and quiet room, away from the hustle and bustle of the household. It is very important that the room is free from draughts. There are many purpose-built whelping boxes available, or you may choose to build your own. Bitches that are heavily in whelp often crumple up the bedding and rearrange it so that they can lie comfortably on it.

The other items that you should assemble before whelping takes place are:

Paper for bedding and old towels.
Olive oil or liquid detergent, which will act as a lubricant if there is an awkward presentation and you need to assist by turning the puppy.
Rough towels to dry off the whelps.

*An ideal whelping box, showing pig rails, although these are not really needed for a Papillon. This box also has an extension, so the puppies have somewhere safe and draught-proof to play when they are up on their feet.*          *Alan V. Walker.*

A clock so that you can time how long the bitch has gone between puppies or how long she has been straining.

A pair of artery forceps to clamp around the cord between the puppy and the afterbirth, if the bitch fails to sever the cord herself.

A hot-water bottle and cover or an electric heat pad for keeping the newly-born whelps warm while the bitch is delivering the next puppy.

A rubbish sack for disposing of soiled newspapers and towels.

A thermometer.

*Mrs Lou Ann King's American bitch, Ken Mar Christmas Holly, with her bumper litter of eight puppies.*

We are always prepared for the bitch to start whelping up to one week before she is due. There are no hard and fast rules about when a bitch will whelp – some are a few days early, some are a few days late, others will produce their litter on the scheduled date. If the bitch is a couple of days late, we usually take her to the vet so that he can monitor her in case of any problems. We had a bitch that whelped a week late with no problems, but it is better to be safe than sorry. We have found that the bitch's temperature normally drops to 99 degrees Fahrenheit about two days before she is actually due to whelp, the normal temperature being 101.5 degrees. Some bitches will refuse food when whelping is imminent, but some never lose their appetite. All bitches are different, so it is a matter of getting to know individual behaviour patterns.

When a bitch is going into labour she will usually appear very restless and be unable to settle. She may also start nesting, tearing up the bedding. She may appear very apprehensive: some will start to shiver, or sometimes a bitch will actually vomit. This is an uncomfortable period which can last from one hour up to twenty-four hours. It is caused by the intro-abdominal pressure, and the contractions at this stage are not very regular and are quite weak. In between these contractions the muscles start to relax, and the vulva and vagina slowly dilate. The bitch often swings round to her back end to investigate, and there is usually evidence of a thick mucus-type discharge, which helps to lubricate the passage ready for the whelp to be born. This is the first

*This Papillon bitch weighs only three pounds, and her puppy, whelped in Denmark, weighed just two ounces.*

stage of labour. The second stage of labour is the actual birth of the whelp. The labour pains now become much stronger and are visible. Sometimes the bitch will lie on her side and push with her hindlegs against the whelping box, and sometimes she will half-sit and push with the contractions. The water bag usually appears first, and by this time the passage has become more dilated and eventually the uterus, cervix and vagina form a wide passage to enable the whelp to be born. The labour pains become stronger and are very regular; sometimes a bitch will whimper as she has a strong contraction. In between the contractions she will try to rest. The whelp gradually makes its way along the passage to the outside world, and in a normal delivery the first thing you will see or feel is the head. Once the head has emerged, the bitch will often rest for a second or two before she expels the rest of the whelp. The whelp itself is attached to the placenta by a cord, sometimes this will not be expelled with the whelp, but will remain inside the bitch until she has had another contraction and expelled it. As soon as the puppy is born, the bitch gets to work and breaks the sac and starts to lick and stimulate the puppy. She will continue doing this, just stopping when a contraction comes. When the afterbirth has been expelled, the bitch will bite through the cord; if she fails to do this, human intervention is called for. Our method is to attach a pair of artery forceps about three inches away from the puppy and clamp them shut, then, using two thumb nails, we gradually break the cord. This is called blunt dissection, and we prefer this method to cutting the cord with a pair of sterilised scissors, as this can cause excessive bleeding. Leave the forceps on for a minute or two and then remove them. The bitch will continue to lick and stimulate the puppy, which will help it to breathe. We allow the bitch to eat one placenta, as it contains useful nutrients, and she will instinctively want to do this. However, we remove all subsequent placentas, wrapping them in newspaper and then putting them in a bag to be burnt or disposed of along with soiled newspapers. Some breeders believe that a bitch should be allowed to eat all the placentas, but in our experience, it gives the bitch severe diarrhoea, which is harmful when she has a litter to rear. We do not take the puppies away from the bitch during whelping as we find she becomes too distressed; but it is important to make sure that they are kept warm and dry at all times. I always think puppies have built-in radar, as they seem to home in on a teat without any trouble. However, if a puppy fails to do this, it will need a little human guidance.

The majority of whelps should emerge head-first, but breach births are fairly common, so there is no need to worry unduly if the puppy comes out hindlegs first. We usually hold on to the back legs with a rough towel – when puppies are still in their sacs they are very slippery – and as the bitch has a contraction, we gently ease the puppy, going round under the bitch towards her chest. Never try to pull a puppy out straight as this could damage the bitch; a little patience is all that is required. When the bitch has expelled the back half of the puppy, she may rest again before expelling the shoulders and head. Sometimes a bitch fails to break the sac, particularly if she is getting tired. In this case, you will need to remove the sac from the puppy's head, and wipe its mouth out with a rough cotton towel – you will be surprised how much rough treatment a puppy can take. The length of time between deliveries can vary from fifteen minutes to a maximum of two hours. After each puppy has been delivered, offer the bitch a drink, as it is important to maintain her fluid level. We use skimmed or semi-skimmed milk. We always serve the milk cold with a couple of drops of liquid calcium and Vitamin D, as warm milk could make

*A two-day old puppy, bred by Mrs J. Lawrence of the Shevarl Papillons. Note that the eyes are closed and there is one small, black spot on the pink-coloured nose. The nose usually takes a few weeks to fully pigment.*

*A puppy at three weeks of age, now looking bright and alert with its eyes open.*

her feel a little drowsy.

When all the puppies have been delivered, let the bitch out to relieve herself. Most bitches hate leaving their puppies for the first few days, so you may have to encourage her to go outside. While she is away, you can clean up the whelping box and put in some fresh, clean bedding. This is also a good time to check the puppies for hare lips, cleft palates, and dewclaws on front and hindlegs. You will also be able to weigh the puppies and find out the number of dogs and bitches in the litter. When the bitch returns, offer her a drink; we do not usually give the bitch anything to eat for the first couple of hours, and then just something light, such as scrambled egg, but we do provide plenty of fluids.

It is always a good idea to ask your vet to check the bitch after she has finished whelping, just in case she has retained a placenta – or even another puppy. If you are not confident that she has delivered all the placentas, or you suspect that there is an unborn puppy, the vet will give the bitch an injection that will encourage her to contract and expel anything that is still in there. Some vets also give a routine antibiotic injection, but be guided by your own vet in this matter. He will also check over the puppies to make sure all is well. Some bitches become quite concerned if someone picks up their puppies, so it is probably preferable to put her outside while the vet is examining the litter. You can also arrange to have the puppies' dewclaws removed when the pups are three days old.

All that is now required is a little peace and quiet in order for the bitch and her puppies to settle, so you must resist the temptation of constantly checking them. Leave the bitch to rest, just making sure she has plenty to drink. For the first twenty-four hours we keep the bitch on a light diet, such as scrambled egg or a little chicken and rice, but do remember to provide plenty of fluids; she may have diarrhoea for a few days, especially if she has eaten the placentas, and it is vital that she does not become dehydrated. After three days, the bitch's appetite increases, and so we normally feed three or four times a day. Also, from the time the bitch begins whelping until the puppies reach four to five weeks of age, we give the bitch liquid calcium and vitamin D (liquid). We add just a small drop into each meal or into the milk she is drinking. The puppies usually take most milk from the bitch between the nineteenth and twenty-seventh days, so the bitch's calcium level can drop quite dramatically at this time, making a calcium supplement essential. The vitamin D is required so that the calcium can be absorbed, and, in fact, most calcium preparations contain vitamin D.

All that the puppies require at this tender age is warmth and milk from their mother. However, there are some danger signs to look out for during whelping and immediately afterwards. If the bitch has strong contractions over a period of one hour with no sign of progress, a puppy could be stuck, or there could be an awkward presentation, and veterinary help will be needed. If contractions cease altogether, the bitch may have gone into uterine inertia, or she may have got so tired that she has given up pushing. Again, veterinary help is required. If the bitch collapses or starts to twitch, you must call the vet immediately. If the bitch has gone into uterine inertia, an injection of pituitary sometimes helps, but failing that, the bitch will need a Caesarian section. Caesarians are needed for a number of different reasons. It could be that the first puppy is very big and the bitch cannot pass it, so obviously the puppies behind it are going to become distressed. A Caesarian would also be needed if there is a very awkward presentation, such as a puppy that is coming down the birth canal sideways, and cannot be expelled. Sometimes a bitch will have one or two puppies quite normally, then she becomes too tired to give birth to the last puppy, so again, a caesarian is needed. It always seems sad when a bitch has produced one or two puppies, but has just not got the energy left for the last puppy. Occasionally, a bitch may not actually be big enough to pass a puppy normally; if this is the case, this should be the first and last litter for the bitch  A caesarian is still a serious operation, although methods have improved greatly over the years. The anaesthetic is kept fairly light, so that, literally, as the last stitch is being put in, the bitch starts to come round. She will normally have started to nurse the puppies by the time you get her back home, although some bitches may need some extra encouragement. If one of our bitches has had a caesarian we always spend the first twenty-four hours with her to make sure everything is alright, and that she has accepted her puppies. Fluids should be offered to her, but only allow her to drink a small amount at a time.

HAND REARING

Sometimes a puppy or a litter will have to be hand-reared, and there are a number of reasons why this can happen. In most cases, the mother does not have enough milk, or the litter has been orphaned. The first essential is for the puppies to be kept very warm, especially if they cannot cuddle up to their mum. Heat can be provided by means of a heated pad or an infra red lamp. The puppies should always feel warm to the touch. A good test is to feel the puppy's feet, and if they feel slightly cool to the touch then the puppy is not getting enough warmth. Secondly, the puppies needs a regular fluid intake. There are a number of milk powders on the market which are designed especially for new-born puppies. However, make sure you follow the manufacturer's instructions to the letter. Never be tempted to add just a little more powder in the hope that this will be good for the puppies; it could have the opposite effect, and in extreme cases it could prove fatal. The milk mixture should be served warm; it should not be too hot, as this could scald the delicate tissue of the puppy's mouth. Equally, it should not be served too cold, as this could lead to stomach upsets. We always feed with a baby's bottle, fitted with a baby-sized teat. Many people think this will be too big to fit into the puppy's mouth, but if you observe puppies feeding from their mothers, you will see that it is not just the nipple that goes into the mouth, but quite a bit of flesh as well.

The puppies will need to be fed every two hours, day and night, which is very time consuming and extremely tiring. The method we use is to place a towel on the lap and put the puppy on this so that it can dig into the towel with its hindlegs. The puppy's mouth will need to be opened manually, making sure that the tongue is at the bottom of its mouth. Then squeeze the end of the teat flat, and put into the pup's mouth. The puppy might pull a few funny faces to start with, but once it realises that it is getting food, it will start to suck enthusiastically. Do not be tempted to over-feed; new-born puppies need fairly small quantities. The golden rule is 'little and often'. We often put a drop of gripe-water in with feed to assist the puppy's digestion.

When the puppy has had its quota of milk, wipe its mouth with a damp piece of cotton wool. Then take another cotton swab, that has been moistened with warm water, and gently pat the puppy's penis or vagina to make it pass water. Finally, take another swab, and using an upward stroking motion, help it to pass faeces. When this has been done, dry the puppy with cotton wool, and apply a little petroleum jelly to prevent the puppy becoming sore. This procedure has to be carried out after every feed, i.e. every two hours day and night. If you are hand-rearing several puppies, you may find that they try to suck each other as they search for their mother's teats, and this can make them very sore. The best course of action may be to separate the puppies, and provide each puppy with a small cardboard box, lined with newspapers and bedding.

Puppies that have been hand-reared will be more vulnerable to infection as they will not have received antibodies from their mother's milk. Extra care must therefore be taken with hygiene, and your vet will advise at what age they should be vaccinated. Hand-rearing a litter can be very rewarding, but it demands a huge investment of time, and it is very easy for things to go wrong, so that you are left with heartbreak, despite all your efforts.

## REARING THE LITTER

If everything goes according to plan and the mother is coping with her puppies, the first three weeks should be fairly straightforward. The puppies should be peaceful and contented, and as far as nutrition is concerned, all they require is the bitch's milk. When the puppies are about ten days old, their eyes start to open, but they are not able to see a lot to begin with.

We weigh the puppies daily for the first four weeks, and this must be done at the same time every day, otherwise you will get fluctuations in the weight pattern. The reason why we weigh our pups is not to see how big they will grow, but in order to detect if a puppy is not getting sufficient nourishment. This can be seen if the weight remains stable, or the puppy starts to lose weight.

We start to wean the puppies when they are about three weeks of age, and this can be quite a stressful time for the puppy, so we try to do it gradually, starting off with mini-mincemeat balls. Our butcher double-minces very lean beef, and we mould a tiny little bit into a very small ball, and pop this into the puppy's mouth. Sometimes they pull quite a face, and then suddenly they realise how good it tastes, and they are all over the place looking for the next one. At this stage, they appear to suck up the food; they have not learned to lap.

If you want to introduce a change, you can use tinned puppy food, which we dilute with a little water, making sure there are no lumps in it. We feed this in a small dish, and the puppies can get into quite a mess, but they have a whale of a time licking each other clean afterwards. To begin with, we feed two meat meals a day. Remember to feed the puppies away from the mother, as she will have no scruples about eating the lot herself! We gradually increase the number of meals to six a day, as we believe in a policy of feeding little and often for growing puppies.

It is a good idea to pick up and handle the puppies each day, right from when they are born, talking to them all the time. This helps to socialise them, and they learn to recognise your voice. When the pups are about four weeks old, they will start to play, wrestling with each other, rushing across the box on wobbly legs, making funny growling noises. At this age, they are very good at reversing, but not as good at going forwards! The bitch will be happy to spend longer periods of time away from the litter, but when she jumps back in, there is a mad scramble from the

*A litter at five weeks of age.*

puppies to hook on to a teat  At about six weeks we try and keep Mum out of the puppies' pen during the day, and put her back in with them at night. Again, there are no hard and fast rules about exactly what age you should do this; it all depends on whether the bitch is enjoying her puppies. However, by the time the puppies are eight weeks old they should be completely weaned off the bitch and fully independent.

The next four weeks are very important for the puppy's social development. This is the time when it should be introduced to all sorts of new noises and different experiences. We have a playpen in the kitchen so the puppies can get used to hearing all of the household noises such as vacuum cleaners and washing machines, and there are always people coming in and out. Puppies of this age will divide their day into mad play sessions alternated with lengthy periods of sleep. If the weather is warm, let the puppies go out into the garden, under supervision of course, or you can take the playpen outside. However, as soon as the puppies tire, bring them in to sleep, as they can get chilled outside. We have a box of toys ranging from the famous dog dollies to squeaky toys, we have a selection of rawhide toys such as shoes and bones, we provide a pair of old tights knotted in about three different places, which  is great for tug of war, and any number

*Sunshoo Imamoonlight Shadow, at eight weeks, with one of the Roe's Maremma Sheepdogs. Playtimes with large and small breeds should always be supervised.*

*Two beautiful red sable puppies, sired by Int. Ch. Lordsrake Fireball.*

*By the time the puppies are 12 weeks, their ears are usually erect.*

of old cardboard boxes for the puppies to play with. One note of caution: just make sure that none of the 'toys' can be swallowed or could be choked on. Puppies are great time-wasters, and no one can resist watching their antics. However, we have to admit that for us, the most magical time is when the puppies are being born, and this miracle has a new fascination every time we witness it.

# Chapter Fifteen

# FIRST AID AND VETERINARY CARE

There is one golden rule that applies in all matters concerning your dog's health and general well-being: if in doubt, contact your veterinary surgeon immediately. We have highlighted some of the more common problems that can occur, and given some tips that may be useful in caring for your Papillon. The first essential is to remember that when you dog is off-colour, it will require warmth, and peace and quiet, in order to rest. Imagine how you would feel if you were suffering from the flu, and every five minutes someone came in to ask how you were, and all you really wanted was to be left alone to sleep. Nursing can play a very important part in aiding a dog's recovery, and this includes: ensuring that the dog is warm and comfortable, following the directions for any medications, and heeding any advice the vet has given. When it comes to food and water, the rule is little and often, and usually a light diet is to be recommended.

When you take your Papillon for its annual booster injection, ask the vet to to give it a general check: listening to the heart, checking the lungs, anal glands, eyes etc. If you have found any lumps and bumps, or are concerned about any aspect of your dog's health, this annual visit provides an ideal opportunity to talk things over – so try to think of any questions you want to ask before you get to the vet's surgery. It may be worth insuring your pet against veterinary treatment. Your vet will usually have details about this, and it may save you considerable expense at a later date. However, the Papillon is, generally speaking, a healthy breed, and hopefully it will not require treatment for anything other than the more common ailments that affect all dogs. We are very lucky that the Papillion is virtually free of hereditary conditions that affect its health, and this should remain the case, so long as all breeders remain vigilant.

ABSCESS

An abscess can be very painful and can sometimes go unnoticed because of the Papillon's long coat. As soon as an abscess is detected it should be bathed carefully in a solution of hot salt-water. This should bring the abscess to a head, and cause it to burst, allowing the pus to drain away. A course of antibiotics may also be necessary to clear up the problem.

ANAL GLANDS

The anal glands are situated on either side of the anus underneath the dog's tail. Sometimes these glands become full or impacted, and they will need to be emptied by your veterinary surgeon. The most usual sign that they are causing discomfort is that the dog will sit down and drag its bottom along on the floor, or it will bite and scratch on top of its back, near the root of its tail.

CHOKING

The signs of choking are gulping, gasping for breath, excessive salivation, and pawing at the mouth. The dog will appear very distressed, but you must try to look in its mouth to see what is causing the obstruction. You may be able to remove the obstruction yourself, but if you are unable to reach it, the dog must be taken to the vet immediately for emergency treatment.

CONSTIPATION

Constipation can sometimes be caused by diet, in which case a slight alteration in food can effect a cure. You could, for instance, include some green vegetables in the normal diet, or a little bran, or a small amount of liver. If the condition persists, seek veterinary advice.

DEAFNESS

Papillons do not seem to suffer with deafness as a congenital abnormality, but sometimes as the dog becomes elderly, partial deafness can occur.

DIARRHOEA

There can be several causes of diarrhoea ranging from nutritional problems to parvovirus, so it is absolutely essential that you act quickly. If it is a nutritional problem, the dog will usually appear bright and happy, but its motions will be very loose or liquid. The first thing to do is to starve the dog for twelve hours, making sure it has access to water, to prevent it becoming dehydrated. You can then feed the dog very small light meals, such as boiled fish and rice, or chicken, but only give a dessertspoon of food every few hours. If you overload the stomach you will be back to square one. If there is any trace of blood in the motions you must contact your vet immediately. Diarrhoea can be caused by a chill, a change of home – this often happens when a puppy goes to its new home – stress, or more serious conditions such as haemorrhagic enteritis, or parvovirus. The condition should clear up rapidly after the dog has been starved, but if it persists, particularly if there is blood in the motions, the dog will require immediate veterinary attention. A virus known as Corona Virus has caused problems in some areas of the USA. In many ways it is similar to parvovirus, but it is not usually fatal. The symptoms of this virus are vomiting and diarrhoea. Veterinary treatment must be sought urgently as the dog quickly becomes dehydrated.

## EARS

The Papillon's ears are its crowning glory, and so it is important that these are kept clean and free from problems. If a dog has trouble with its ears it will either keep scratching its ear and shaking its head or it will hold its head to one side. It is usually best to take your dog to the vet in this instance, as you could cause considerable harm if you try and poke around in the ear. The vet will use an auroscope to have a look in the ear to see what is causing the problem. It could be ear mites or canker, in which case the dog will require a course of drops to put in the ear. The problem could be caused by a foreign body such as a grass seed, and this will need removing, or it could set up an infection that will need treatment with antibiotics.

Loss of hair and fringes on the ear can be a frustrating problem in Papillons that are competing in the show ring. The dog does not appear to scratch the ear, but when it is being brushed and combed, or if it is being bathed, the hair just seems to come away. Sometimes you can see greasy flakes of skin, and sometimes there is a hardening of the ear margin, but this is not always the case. The condition is caused by Ear Mange Dermatosis. The best treatment is to wash the ears twice a week with a special preparation, which your vet will supply. There is also a preparation, called Ceanal, made for humans which some vets recommend, and this would be available from a pharmacy.

## EYES

Discharges from the eyes can have several causes; probably the most common is when the tear ducts become blocked and the eyes 'weep' and run over. As the Papillon is a small dog, the tear ducts are also small and do become easily blocked with debris. If you detect any sign of trouble, just bathe and clean the eye with damp cotton-wool (cotton). However, if there is a coloured discharge which is a greeny-yellow colour, it usually indicates an infection. This will mean a trip to the vet to get some antibiotic ointment. Very occasionally, due to damage to the eye, an ulcer will appear. This needs veterinary treatment. Some vets stitch the third eyelid over to assist the healing process, but in this situation you must be guided by what your vet recommends.

## HEART PROBLEMS

If your Papillon is given an annual check-up by your vet, any heart problems should be detected at an early stage. The heart can become less efficient with old age; the first sign the owner will notice is a harsh dry cough, or the dog may become out of breath and lethargic. The vet will be able to carry out tests to diagnose the problem, and there is now a lot of medication available to treat the condition.

## HEATSTROKE

Heatstroke is a most distressing condition, and extreme caution must be taken to ensure that your Papillon does not become over-heated. Never ever leave your dog in car on a sunny day, without sufficient ventilation. If you have to leave your dog, make sure it is only for a very short period. It can be quite a chilly day outside, but inside the car in the full sun it does not take long for the air to heat up and for the dog to literally cook. So if it is a sunny day, and you don't need to take your dog with you, leave it at home.

When a dog is suffering from heatstroke it becomes very distressed, and highly excitable. It may foam at the mouth; its eyes look as if they are going to pop. This can be followed by collapse and death. Immediate first aid must be applied: the dog must be placed in the cool, and if there is a supply of cold water, immerse the dog, leaving its head clear of the water. Icepacks can be applied – the aim is to cool the dog as quickly as possible, with whatever means available – and then seek immediate veterinary attention This is a condition that can be avoided with careful management of your dog.

## INGUINAL HERNIAS

These are found in the groin, and can be located on both sides of the groin. They can occur in dogs and bitches, and you should be advised by your vet as to whether an operation is required to repair them. It is not advisable to use dogs or bitches affected by this condition for breeding.

## KENNEL COUGH

This is an unfortunate name, as most people think their dogs can only catch the condition if the dog is boarded in a kennel. Kennel cough is highly infectious; it is passed from dog to dog, and so dogs can catch it in any situation. However, in kennels the risk of the infection spreading are far higher, and so any dog that is coughing should be isolated. The condition itself is not usually too serious. It lasts for a variable length of time: the dog may be better in a week, but it can persist for a longer period. Sometimes a small amount of cough mixture such as Benylin Expectorant, which is made for humans, can help alleviate the symptoms. The vet will normally prescribe a course of antibiotics to prevent secondary infections, but do not take your dog into a waiting room full of dogs, otherwise the infection could spread. Special care must be taken with young puppies and older dogs, as in severe cases kennel cough can lead to pneumonia.

## KIDNEY PROBLEMS

The usual signs of kidney failure are an excessive thirst and frequent passing of water. If you notice these symptoms, take your dog to the vet, and if possible, try to take a urine sample. This should be collected in a clean bottle, and the vet will test it immediately, which will save time and aid the diagnosis.

## LIVER DISEASE

Unfortunately all liver problems are usually serious, so if you suspect a problem, do not delay in seeking veterinary advice. The first sign is usually jaundice; this can be detected by a yellowing of the white of the eye and of the membrane lining the eye, and also yellowing inside the mouth. Other symptoms are vomiting and passing of highly coloured urine.

## POISONING

Depending on the poison, the symptoms can vary from vomiting to muscular spasm, and if Warfarin has been eaten, bleeding from the gums can occur. Obviously, you must contact the vet without delay. If you know what poison the dog has eaten, or in some cases walked through and then licked his pads, make a note of it, or take the packet or bottle with you to the vet. It is extremely important that the right antidote is given as quickly as possible, as this could save your dog's life.

## SCRATCHING

Scratching can be due to any number of things, but you should first check the most obvious causes. Examine the dog's coat to see if there is any evidence of fleas or flea-dirts. If you find your dog has fleas, a medicated bath and regular use of a topical anti-parasitic treatment is usually very effective. Scratching can also be caused by sarcoptic mange. In this instance, the skin will be reddened and the condition will need treatment from the vet.

## SNORTING

New owners can become quite concerned about this condition, although there is no cause for alarm. The dog stands fairly rigidly, and pushes its head forward and takes very deep breaths, making a snorting type of noise. It very often happens when the dog is excited, and it is not usually serious, although new owners are sometimes concerned about it. It can be alleviated by putting your hand over the dog's nose so that it has to breathe through its mouth. However, if you are worried, consult your vet.

## STINGS

If your dog is stung in the mouth or the throat, immediate veterinary attention must be sought, as the dog will need an anti-histamine injection. If your dog is stung by a bee, try to remove the sting  with tweezers, and then apply bicarbonate of soda. For wasp stings, apply a little vinegar to the affected area. In some regions of the USA dogs can become afflicted with Heartwood, which is caught from a mosquito biting a dog. The dog then becomes thin, it usually  drops coat and become quite wheezy. Veterinary treatment is required for this, and some owners keep their dogs on medication to prevent them becoming afflicted.

## STRESS

Stress is not necessarily an illness in itself, but it can lead to health problems. For instance, when a puppy changes home it may well suffer from a tummy upset. This is because it has so much to get used to: new surroundings, new noises, new faces, and sometimes a change of diet. This can also happen to a dog attending its first show; it may become stressed by all the dogs and people milling about. This is not something to worry about, but all dog owners should be aware that it can happen and should try to introduce their dog to new situations as tactfully as possible.

## TICKS

Ticks can be quite easily picked up by dogs when they are exercised in country where sheep have been grazing. Do not be tempted to try to pull the tick off the dog, as this will probably leave the head attached to the dog, and this could result in an abscess. The best way to remove the whole tick is to dab it with surgical spirit or spray it with a topical insecticide, and then it should be quite easy to extract it.

## TEETH

If a dog is suffering from toothache it will normally hold its head on one side, or it may try and paw its mouth. If the dog has a tooth abscess, its face will probably be swollen, and it will need attention from the vet. Unfortunately, quite a number of Papillons lose some teeth quite early in life, and so it is important to ensure that the teeth are kept clean and free of calculus. This can be done by regular cleaning of the teeth with canine toothpaste, using one of the special toothbrushes that are available in some pet shops. You can ask your vet to scale the dog's teeth, but unfortunately, this necessitates a general anaesthetic. Make sure your dog has plenty of things to chew on, such as the raw-hide dog chews and hard biscuits, but avoid bones. These can splinter very easily and can get stuck in a dog's throat, and if a splinter is swallowed it could cause internal damage.

## TRAVEL SICKNESS

Many dogs are never travel-sick, but unfortunately some are bad travellers. Some dogs are actually sick, others just drool and salivate. The best way to avoid this problem is to take your dog out in the car as often as possible. Start by going on short trips, and then gradually extend the length of the journey. When you arrive at your destination, let the dog have a short walk or play, so that it associates going out in the car with something pleasurable. Do not feed your dog immediately before you take it out in the car. If the problem persists, you can try travel sickness tablets, that are available from the vet. However, some of these can make a dog very drowsy for the rest of the day, so try and persevere with the regular trips in the car, and hopefully, this will eventually solve the problem.

UMBILICAL HERNIA

This is a hernia which, as it name implies, is near the umbilicus. It often happens when the puppy is born. Your vet will advise as to whether an operation is required.

UNDESCENDED TESTICLES

If a male dog has no testicles descended it is known as a cryptorchid; if he has only one testicle descended, it is known as a monorchid. In most cases the testicles should have descended by the time the dog is about nine months old. If the dog reaches eighteen months old and still has a retained testicle, you should speak to your vet to see if an operation is necessary, as sometimes retained testicles can become tumorous.

VOMITING

Continuous vomiting needs immediate veterinary attention, as the dog can become dehydrated quite quickly. Occasionally a dog will regurgitate its meal – this is nothing to worry about. A dog will sometimes bring up some yellowish bile, which can be caused by a minor stomach upset.

WORMS

The roundworm, which is the most common worm to infest dogs, is, as its name suggests, round in shape; it varies in length and is white or cream in colour. All puppies should be regularly wormed against roundworms, and adults should be wormed as a precaution every six months, or if they are infested with fleas. A dog should also be wormed if it has suffered a prolonged bout of illness; but wait at least a month after all the symptoms have disappeared, so you are sure the dog is fully fit again. The signs of a roundworm burden in a puppy are a voracious appetetite, a dull coat, and the pup often looks pot-bellied. An adult with roundworms tends to look thin and pinched, and its coat looks dull and lacklustre. There are a number of different worming treatments on the market, so it is best to seek the advice of your vet. Occasionally, Papillons suffer from tapeworms. These look like small, flat grains of rice and are usually to be found near the anus. Again, your vet will recommend a suitable worming product.

# APPENDIX

## FURTHER READING

If you are a devotee of the Papillon, there are several books and publications that will be of particular interest.

*Papillon and Phalene Champions from 1925*
By Carolyn Roe
Privately published, available direct from author (01522 686737
david@roesunshoo.freeserve.co.uk).
Photographs and pedigrees of all British and Phalene Champions.

*The Papillon Handbook*
By Peggy and Bob Roberts
Published by Foyles.
This is from the Dog Lovers Library, and sadly, it is out of print. However, it is still very much in demand, and it is expensive to buy if you are lucky enough to come across a copy.

*The Butterfly Dog*
By Clarice Waud and Pat Challis.
Published by Nimrod Press.
A paperback book that is full of useful information.

*The Papillon Butterfly Dog*
By Clarice Waud and Mark Hutchings.
Published by Nimrod Press.
This is a definitive reference book for the breed.

*Small Dog Obedience Training*
By Alex Foreman.
Published by Nimrod Press
This is a very useful book on the training of toy dogs for basic competitive obedience. The Papillon is featured, highlighting Mrs Foreman and her Bordercott Papillons.

*Papillon and Phalene*
By Suzanne Tamm.
Published by Ica Dokforlag Vasteraf
This is written in Swedish, but it is well worth acquiring as it has some beautiful photographs.

*The Papillon Scrapbook*
This is a selection of articles first published by the Papillon Club of America in their club magazine.

*Toy Dogs*
By Clarice Waud and Mark Hutchings.
Published by Nimrod Press
This is a comprehensive history covering all breeds in the Toy Group.

*The Hutchinsons Dog Encyclopedia*
This runs into three volumes, and is out of print, but it can be found in bookstalls specialising in old books. There is an extensive article on the Papillon, with some lovely photographs.

*Dogs and How to Breed Them*
By Hilary Harmer.
Published by J. Gifford.
This is an excellent book on breeding, and has plenty of illustrations, which makes the text easy to understand.

*Dog Shows and Show Dogs*
By Catherine Sutton.
Published by K and R Classics.
This is a very detailed book and is lavishly illustrated.

*Dog And Cat Nutrition*
Edited by A.T.B. Edney
Published by the Pergammon Press.
This is a must for the serious breeder as it gives a comprehensive guide on all aspects of nutrition.

*Canine Terminology*
By Harold R. Spira.
Published by David and Charles.
We have found this very useful as a reference, and the illustrations are invaluable.

*The Kennel Club's Illustrated Breed Standards.*
Published by Bodley Head.
This is a bible for everyone in the show world as it gives all the British Breed Standards, plus an introduction to each breed.

## USEFUL NAMES AND ADDRESSES

### NATIONAL KENNEL CLUBS

The English Kennel Club,
1-5 Clarges Street,
Piccadilly,
London,
W1Y 8AB


The Irish Kennel Club,
Fottrell House,
Unit 36,
Greenmount Office Park,
Dublin, 6

The American Kennel Club,
51 Madison Avenue,
New York,
NY 10010

The Canadian Kennel Club,
89 Skyway Avenue,
Etobicoke,
Ontario,
M9W 6R4

Australian National Kennel Council,
Royal Show Grounds,
Ascot Vale,
Victoria

Germany
Verband fur das Deutche Hundewessen (VDH),
Westfalendamm 174,
Postfach 1390,
D4600 Dortmund, Germany.

Switzerland
Schweizerische Kynologische Gesellschaft,
Langgasstrasse 8,
Postfach 8217,
CH-3001,
Bern,  Switzerland

Denmark
Dansk Kennelklub,
Pakvej 1,
Jersie Strand,
2680,
Solad Strand,
Denmark

Sweden
Svenska Kennelklubben,
Norrbyvagan 30,
Box 11043,
16111 Bromma,
Sweden

Kennel Union of Southern Africa,
6th Floor,
Bree Castle,
68 Bree Street,
Cape Town 8001,
S. Africa

## BREED CLUBS

AMERICA

There are Breed Clubs in a number of States, but all up-to-date information can be obtained from:

The Papillon Club of America,
Roseann Fucillo,
2600 Kennedy Blvd,
Jersey City,
NJ (07306)

UK

The Papillon Club,
Secretary, Mrs C. Allward Chebsey,
44 Gilbert Road,
Lichfield,
Staffordshire
WS13 6AX

Northern and Eastern Papillon Club,
Secretary, Mr J. Edson,
The Butterflies,
18 Mill Lane,
Ryther,
North Yorkshire
LS24 9EG

The Papillon Club of Scotland,
Secretary, Mr E. Whitehill,
117 Cheviot Road,
Kirkaldy,
Fife,
Scotland
KY2 5YP

The South Wales Papillon Club,
Secretary, Miss K. Farrell,
Oakdene,
Green Lane,
Staines,
Middlesex
JW18 3LX

Papillon Breed Council,
Secretary, Mr E. Whitehill,
117 Cheviot Road,
Kirkaldy,
Fife,
Scotland
KY2 6BE